MEMOIR

OF

PRISCILLA CADWALLADER.

"The Lord is their strength, and He is the *saving strength* of His anointed."

PHILADELPHIA:

PUBLISHED FOR THE BOOK ASSOCIATION OF FRIENDS,

BY T. ELLWOOD ZELL,

Nos. 17 and 19 South Sixth Street.

1862.

PREFACE.

Believing there was a debt due to the memory of our beloved friend PRISCILLA CADWALLADER, this little labor of love has been performed, with the desire also that the remembrance of her humility and devotion may encourage others to a like submission to the regulating and qualifying power of Truth, that so there may be a succession of standard-bearers, who can say as she said, both by precept and practice, "I am not ashamed of the gospel of Christ, for it is the power of God unto salvation, to every one that believeth."

J. J.

MEMOIR.

It is well to bring to our remembrance the character and virtuous lives of those faithful servants and handmaids of the Most High who have passed away from this state of being. Future generations, and many at the present time, may derive strength and profit from the perusal of the lives of those who have endeavored, through the trials and discouragements that attended them here, to walk worthy of the vocation to which they were called.

"Who is blind, but my servant, or deaf as my messenger that I sent," (Isaiah xlii. 19,) seems especially applicable in connection with the religious engagements and movements of that dignified minister of the gospel, the late Priscilla Cadwallader.

Her writings having been destroyed during her absence from home, and no connected account of her life preserved, we are unable to represent her labors and exercises as fully as would be desirable; but the *fragments* gathered from various sources, will, we think, prove instructive and interesting.

She was born in North Carolina, the 10th of 7th mo., 1786. Her father, Matthew Coffin, was a native of Nantucket, and her mother, Hannah Coffin, formerly Mendenhall, was from Chester County, Pa. Her mother died when she was quite young. Her father was well known and much respected as a man of superior judgment; he was for many years an Elder of Springfield Monthly Meeting, N. C., and endeavored to give his children the blessing of a guarded education.

Priscilla's school opportunities were limited, but owing to the advantages of parental home instruction, she had read the Bible through when only six years of age. Her early fondness for serious reading and the society of those much older than herself, were the peculiar characteristics of her childhood. Her perceptive and reasoning powers were large and early developed, and she availed herself of all the means of study furnished from books and other sources. The great volume of Nature was marvellously unfolded to her comprehension, and she became early in life interested in Geology, Mineralogy and Natural History. Her acquaintance with these sciences was remarkable, and afforded throughout her life an unfailing source of enjoyment. She was in a great measure self-educated, and in after years, during the long journeys of many hundred miles, taken in the prosecution of her religious engagements, when not under the immediate pressure of religious exercise, she would sometimes pour forth the rich abundance of her mental treasury, dwelling with beautiful interest upon the outward evidences of her heavenly Father's love. To her mind there was no contradiction in any of His revelations to man, whether communicated by books, or unfolded through natural objects. She looked "through Nature up to Nature's God," and where she could not fathom, "learned to trust."

In 1811 she married Jabez Hunt, son of Nathan Hunt, of North Carolina, a member of the Society of Friends, and in about two years was left a widow in limited circumstances, with one child.

In 1814 she removed to Indiana, then almost a wilderness, and settled on a farm which her father purchased for her within the limits of what is now known as the Blue River settlement of Friends. She and her daughter were recommended by certificate to Lick Creek Monthly Meeting. Blue River Monthly Meeting was not at that time established. Priscilla Hunt was afterwards one of its first members.

Her first appearance as a minister was in 1815, and in about two years her ministry was acknowledged by her Monthly Meeting. Before she was thirty-seven years of age she had visited in gospel love all the meetings of Friends then established in America. She afterwards travelled extensively in Truth's service, again visiting all the meetings composing the Yearly Meetings of Philadelphia, New York, Genesee, Indiana, Ohio and Baltimore, as well as many meetings in Canada. The records of Blue River Monthly Meeting show she was liberated for the aforesaid extensive journeys by minutes issued in 1829, 1839, 1846, 1850 and 1853.

In the testimony gathered from different sources, the extraordinary character of her ministry is repeatedly alluded to. Some instances wherein she was very closely introduced into individual states, may appear almost incredible, but a history of the ministry in our Society abundantly shows that in addition to the *immediate* and powerful communings of the Most High with the souls of his rational creatures, by which they are made to know the things that make for their own peace, there is sometimes conferred a gift, which introduces its possessor into close sympathy with other minds.* The possession of this gift, in the degree exhibited by the subject of this memoir is *rare.* Other minds must not therefore estimate their spiritual advancement by the possession or non-possession of it—doing so, would but discourage the humble traveller, in whose experience there has been nothing of this character, and lead others to overlook the usually simple, beautiful and harmonious promptings to goodness, which are common to all, while looking for that which is supernatural.

It was an important part of the mission of our beloved friend, to call the people home to the eternal in-speaking Word, as she would say on divers occasions, "This is all I have to depend on, and all I have to call others unto.

---

* In the 12th chapter of Corinthians, allusion is made to gifts of this nature.

It is in the heart of man that the Lord God of Israel speaks to his people." In the prosecution of her extensive religious services, she was an example of patient waiting for the word of command. She was often a silent laborer, feeling there was a time to speak and a time to keep silence, and as in child-like simplicity her dependence was placed upon the only wise Counsellor, "she was a minister when silent, and impressive and powerful when engaged in vocal testimony."

Perhaps few, in their daily living, have so generally manifested a desire to walk closely by the pattern shown, or were more concerned to wait for the evidence of right direction. This retiredness of spirit may be said to have been her marked characteristic; even when in company, though her natural disposition was cheerful and social, it was not unusual for her to be so abstracted as to be scarcely conscious of what was going on around her. She frequently said, her safety consisted in this introversion of mind.

She was careful never to participate in party strife, and her feelings saluted all in Gospel love without respect to differences of opinion. In her social minglings she discouraged all species of detraction, and if needful bore a vocal testimony against this pernicious practice: when she could not check such conversation, nor avoid hearing it, she would retire to her chamber, where much of her time between meetings was spent in meditation or in reading the Scriptures. Owing in part to the records of Blue River Monthly Meeting being in possession of Orthodox Friends, and therefore difficult of access, little data has been obtained of the early years of her religious service. The few memoranda and letters that have been preserved by her travelling companions will show the character of her gospel labors. One remarkable instance of the exercise of the gift of discernment, which was bestowed upon our friend, is thus related by a member of Blue River Quarterly Meeting as having occurred in the summer of 1822.

It refers to a man who had for many years apparently rejected the fundamental truths of the Christian religion.

"One morning, he said, 'I am 60 years old to-day, I will go to Quaker Meeting.' He accordingly went to the meeting that Priscilla Hunt attended. After the meeting was gathered, P. arose and spoke as follows:—'I am 60 years old to-day, and I will go to Quaker meeting.' These words were spoken this morning by one who I believe is now present. She then minutely described his state, and as arguments would arise in his mind, she refuted them, as pointedly as if she had heard him speak (as he afterwards said) until he was entirely disarmed of them all. She then sat down. After a few minutes, she arose again, and stated, the person was disarmed of all the false arguments, wherewith he had fortified himself, and unless he solicits a revival of them, he may live in the way that will lead to peace and salvation. On next meeting day he was again at meeting, and when Priscilla kneeled in supplication, he also kneeled, much to the astonishment of the audience. After meeting he made known the situation of his mind, and after some time he requested to be joined in membership with Friends."

Rachel Johnson, who was Priscilla's companion at that time, confirms the foregoing statement, and says that shortly after the communication, Priscilla had a private interview with the individual, and information has since been received that he continues to be a firm believer in the principles of Christianity, and attributes his conversion to the above mentioned sermon.

On the 4th of Seventh month, 1822, Priscilla Hunt, accompanied by her father, Matthew Coffin and Rachel Johnson, attended Goose Creek Meeting, Virginia. This appears to have been the commencement, of her first visit this side of the Alleghany mountains, as a minister. Bernard Taylor, of Loudon Co., Virginia, took her father's place as companion, and was with her several months. They appear to have travelled under the feeling of Gospel fellowship, visiting the meetings pretty generally in Virginia and Maryland, and many in Pennsylvania and New Jersey.

During this visit, our friend, in one of her public testimonies, addressed an individual in high standing, intimating that he was in the path of error. After meeting, as they were going to the place where they expected to dine, Priscilla asked the Friend who drove them, if he would be willing to drive a short distance out *another* road, to which she pointed. He replied, "yes, where dost thou want to go?" Priscilla answered, "I do not know, but I want thee to drive on." They went on about half a mile, when P. requested they might stop at the next house. Their driver queried, "dost thou know who lives there?" P. said, "No, but please drive up." The Friend of the house came out to the carriage, when Priscilla immediately spoke to him thus: "I believe thou hast taken to thyself what I said in meeting to-day. *It does not belong to thee*, and I have thought it right to come and tell thee so." The Friend replied, thou hast taken a great burden off my mind—one I could hardly bear." His manner manifested his great distress. He was an humble, meek-spirited man, and easily discouraged, and being in a low spot, had let in the reasoner, and was made to believe a lie. Hence he had taken to himself the searching testimony that belonged to another. The Friend who drove, said, his faith was weak and had almost failed, when first told to go, *he knew not where*, but when he had such clear evidence that Priscilla had been rightly guided, and looked upon her countenance radiant with divine intelligence, he could no longer doubt her mission.

During the years 1823 and '24, our Friend made a general visit through most of the middle and eastern States and Upper Canada. The first information we have in connection with this journey is her attendance of a meeting held in Arch street meeting house, Philadelphia, in 2d mo., 1823, when she delivered the following searching communication :

"Men who work hard all day for nothing, are truly to be pitied. My lips have been sealed in silence since I have been in this meeting, but not through the fear of man. I have been viewing as in the vision of Light, men digging a pit, and in making it large enough to contain the Lord's servants that pass by that way, I have seen that they have undermined their own habitations. Thus the snare they would lay for the weary traveller's feet, they have fallen into themselves. Over this pit I have seen spacious buildings, which being undermined must fall in the vortex of this destructive, horrible pit. You toil hard all day long, and instead of the sweet reward of peace for your labors, you lay down your heads at night in anguish of spirit, a clear evidence how hard the master is you serve. You have forms, but deny the power of the Eternal Word, which was in the beginning, which was with God, and which was God. In Him was life; and the life was the light of men. Like the persecuting Jews of old, after stripping the body of Jesus, you contend for the raiment, little heeding that when torn from that prepared body, healing virtue no longer remained in it. Still you contend for the very fragments of the garments, and cast lots for the vesture, to the utter neglect of the living eternal substance. That spiritual life you (Pharisee-like) persecute, and would even nail to the cross. But your power is limited; not a bone can you break. Oh, I am weary; the spirit within me is weary of high profession. For religion, is substituted opinion. Hence contentions, divisions and subdivisions; and in blind zeal and self-will the blessed Truth and its advocates are judged down, and the feet of the messengers are turned another way. I have seen the Gospel trumpet laid down in this city. False alarms have been sounded here and believed. True alarms have been sounded and not believed. These things I brought not with me; you will judge of their correctness. Now beloveds, in that Gospel love which I feel flowing in me, and which embraces you all, and all the human family without distinction, have I endeavored simply to lay before you these things, desiring that none may take them to themselves but those to whom they may apply. For I believe there is a remnant who go mourning on their way, and who, on the wings of redeeming Love, will be made to soar above all the devices of cruel man."

In 4th mo., 1823, she attended Philadelphia Yearly Meeting, and visited most of the meetings in the neighborhood of that city. John Ward was her companion at that time. His memorandums show that they travelled in unbroken unity. He says:

"Our spirits have been often baptized together in the work and service to which we have been called, and I have to commemorate the gracious dealings of Israel's shepherd, who hath led us about, and instructed us and preserved us through many trials."

Of one meeting he says:

"This was a great meeting; not in numbers, but in *the power* that attended. Our dear friend was favored with gospel authority, and Truth reigned over all."

Again he says:

"Attended meeting at B. Sat down poor and pennyless—neither purse nor scrip, but through the aboundings of that Love, which is both ancient and new, our minds were favored to rise above every obstruction, and we had a memorable meeting. Our dear friend was eminently furnished with matter, and there was a precious opening to declare the doctrines of the Gospel to a very large assembly. The meeting concluded with solemn supplication, that all might arise and come forth from a fallen state, and freely partake of the joys of God's salvation."

"Attended meeting at R. This was a precious, comfortable time. We had, I think, a clear evidence that the Lord hath not forsaken his people, for divine Love was as a canopy over us, and all seemed to be gathered and centered to the great First Cause. Our dear Friend had to travail through deep exercise to minister to several states; I united in the fellowship of the Gospel with her close searching testimony. The meeting was held, I believe, to the edification of the people, and closed with much solemnity."

We have the following notice from a Friend in attendance at two meetings held at Wilmington, Delaware, about this time:

"I attended meeting on First-day morning, which was very large, and many present not of our Society. Priscilla Hunt commenced her discourse by observing that she 'knew a woman could not preach, neither could a man—that is, *preach the everlasting gospel*, though they might deliver an eloquent discourse.' She then proceeded to show the equal authority of woman with man to preach the gospel. She mentioned that she had read the Scriptures attentively from Genesis to Revelations, and had never found any prohibition, but quite the contrary. That Deborah, Miriam and Huldah were prophetesses of the Lord; also that Anna is mentioned in the New Testament as a prophetess, and Phebe is spoken of by the Apostle as a servant of the church, and Priscilla as his helper in Christ Jesus. She said she knew that the same Apostle commanded that women should keep silence in the church, and if they will learn any thing they must ask their husbands at home. This was in reference to women who made impertinent inquiries in the assemblies of the people, but could no more be intended to prohibit woman's preaching, than to prohibit their receiving religious instruction except from their husbands at home, and if it were to be thus construed, the poor women would be in a miserable state, as not one-third part of mankind was capable of affording them religious instruction. She then added, (supposing it could have been so intended,) that the command could only have been given to those women who had husbands. She then remarked that she knew not why she was thus led; it certainly was not intended as an apology for her preaching, for she considered it beneath the dignity of a gospel minister to apologise for what she had to communicate. The remainder of her discourse was on humility and love. She rose a second time and remarked, she did not wish to be misunderstood when she said it was beneath the dignity of the gospel for a minister to apologise. There was no dignity belonging to the creature; *that* must be humbled and brought low.

" I afterwards learned there were a number of persons present who disclaimed the authority of women to preach, and two young men particularly, who had said, on the evening previous, they did not intend to go to meeting, as they thought women had no right to preach.

" In the afternoon meeting P. sat perhaps one hour and a half, the greater part of the time apparently under great exercise of mind. When she rose, she repeated the text, " Oh that my head were waters and mine eyes a fountain of tears, that I might weep day and night for the slain of the daughters of my people." She then said she had brought nothing with her, but what she had received there she dare not take away, and must tell them that the Truth was groaning under oppression,—that there was something among them, which, if not abandoned, would produce a famine in the land. She exhorted them to try the matter in themselves, and if found true, listen to the language of the Spirit, Come away, come away from these things. Having spoken at considerable length she sat down, and after some time rose again and said, she had heard nothing respecting them, but she believed there was an attempt to explain the Scriptures in man's own wisdom; she knew not whether among the gay or the plain, but that they who were striving to draw most to their side, might be compared to those who divided the garments of Jesus and cast lots for his vesture."

Many of the families of Friends in Philadelphia were visited about this time. From our remembrance of the engagement, the visits were made somewhat informally, as her mind was arrested and drawn to different places. Very many instances might be brought into view, as evidences of the spirit of discernment, and even of prophecy, with which she was gifted. Several are now living whose paths through life were at that time clearly pointed out by her. They are living witnesses of the truth of her prophetic declarations. James Walton, formerly of Byberry, Pa., was her companion in these visits. He also accompanied her in an extensive journey through Pennsylvania, New York, and Upper Canada. From his notes we make copious extracts, to show not only the character of her religious services, but also the difficulties then attendant on a journey of 2400 miles—so different from the easy and rapid means of transportation now afforded by rail-road.

Extracts from the Journal of James Walton.

"I left my habitation in Byberry on Fourth day, the 7th of the 5th month, 1823, in company with Priscilla Hunt and Rachael Johnson, (who were on a religious visit to the meetings of Friends within the compass of Baltimore, Pennsylvania, New York, and Rhode Island Yearly Meetings,) and attended our Quarterly Meeting of ministers and elders held at Horsham, and next day the Quarterly Meeting, in both of which our friend P. H. was silent.

"9th.—Had a large meeting at Abington, wherein our dear friend was livingly opened in the power of the Gospel, to set things close home to individuals and the meeting at large; it ended well.

"12th.—Attended a meeting appointed at Wakefield; a memorable one to me and perhaps many others; although I had, before I set out, a more full evidence of its being right for me to give up to go this journey than has been usual for me to see or feel, yet I now began to be tried about leaving my family so long to go so far as Canada. Although I could not get over the feelings I had witnessed on the occasion, yet on entering that house I felt a strong desire that I might have some further evidence in that meeting of its being right, if it was so, which was granted to my astonishment and satisfaction. The evidence furnished gave full proof to my mind of my dear friend's mission and the propriety of my present engagement. All doubts were dispersed, and my mind set at liberty from my concern respecting affairs at home.

"13th.—Attended Newtown meeting. Our beloved friend had hard work among them. Some close things to point out, especially to one individual who was much affected. Experienced Friends thought it a favored time.

"14th.—Attended their meeting at the Falls, where there were two marriages. A large collection of different denominations was present, to whom our dear friend was enabled to preach the Gospel with life and power. After a feeling supplication the meeting concluded.

"15th.—This morning the individual who had been so particularly spoken to at Newtown called to see us, and informed us that he had wished to have an opportunity with P. H., but having been at the meeting yesterday and had time since to digest the matter, he had been satisfied without, but wished to be a little in her company and attend the meeting this day at Pennsbury. He then informed us of his situation for some time back, which exactly corresponded with what had been described at Newtown.

"18th.—First of the week, we took a solemn leave of my family, and attended Middletown meeting, which was very large; here the Gospel was preached in Divine Authority, and things opened in a very close manner to some, after which a solemnizing and heart-tendering supplication under a renewed and feeling sense that the Gospel trumpet was yet sounded among us.

"7th of the 6th month and 1st of the week, we attended a large and crowded meeting at Muncey, where our beloved friend Priscilla Hunt, was powerfully opened in the life to search the camp as with a lighted candle; it was a memorable day; the Gospel flowed freely, and many were sensibly affected. Dined at Mercy Ellis', and went on toward Elkland, and lodged at a house of entertainment.

"8th.—Towards evening had a meeting with the few Friends of that place and others, which was a comfortable opportunity.

"9th.—Returned back to Muncey. This route has exceeded any thing I have yet seen, for dangerous travelling, over the Alleghany mountains and through the wilderness woods, stumps, rocks and stones; some places it appeared as if we must be cast overboard, but through all this difficulty our women remained unmoved, entirely composed, and showed no symptoms of alarm; we lodged at a tavern on our way to Fishing Creek.

"10th.—Had a meeting at Fishing Creek; I thought a heavenly one. The Gospel was preached by our dear friend with great power, and after a solemn supplication the meeting closed."

"16th.—Set out for New York State; the country very rough and the roads bad; crossed the river Susquehanna at Crane's Ferry, and passed down it to Oswego; dined on our way at a tavern, and lodged at a public house six miles from Oswego.

"17th.—Passed on through Danby, a little village, to Ithica, where we dined at a very good tavern. From Friendsville to this place, 54 miles; from thence to Hector, 13 miles, over a very rough road.

"18th.—Attended Hector meeting, it being small and our beloved friend very unwell. She was not so large in testimony as at some other times, yet we had the evidence of its being right: a comfortable solemnity was over the meeting, but it was one of those times when it was especially necessary to look for the stepping-stones. Dined at Caleb Carman's, and went on to Elmira, a distance of 20 miles, through a wooden country and excessive bad roads; here we passed some of the finest pine timber that I have ever seen; on our way we travelled near the Cayuga Lake for some distance, halted at what is called the Johnson settlement, took tea at a tavern, and arrived at our destined port at about 10 o'clock; the people having gone to bed, we were admitted, after some hesitation on the part of the woman of the house, the man being from home. She felt some doubts about letting strangers in so late at night; however as soon as we made known our business and who we were, she very soon opened her house and took us in. Next day, 19th, at 3 o'olock, afternoon, we had a meeting of a mixed multitude; it was held in a barn, and was a precious opportunity. Our friend P. H. had much to do among them in opening the doctrines of the Gospel. Some deep things were opened with great clearness to their satisfaction.

"20th.—Returned to Hector, and lodged at Charles Carman's.

"21st.—Passed through a handsome part of the country to the Cayuga Lake, and crossed it in a horse-boat, three miles wide at this place; from thence to Thomas Hutchinson's; lodged and were kindly entertained. Next day was first of the week and 22d of the month—a day to be remembered by many. Our dear friend was enabled through the aid of Him who laid this concern upon her, and who I believe put her forth and is going before her, to sound an alarm. Being furnished with a clear sight and sense of things among them, she was enabled to point them out in a very clear manner, to the great satisfaction of the sincere-hearted. It was a good meeting.

"6th mo. 23d.—Jos. Frost went with us to Salmon Creek, Semphronius, and Skaneateles; all these were favored meetings; the everlasting Gospel was preached with Divine authority. On our way from this place we halted at Aurora, where we expected to lodge, but our friend P. H. felt a stop as I was preparing to help her out of the wagon. She said it would not do to lodge there. We therefore went on and reached another port some time after dusk. We here found no notice of a meeting had been spread or sent into the neighborhood. The omission was by accident. It was well that we attended to P. H.'s feelings, otherwise we should have lost a day and deranged our prospects. I have found it safest to consult her feelings on all occasions respecting our movements. Notice was immediately spread that evening.

"26th.—Attended the meeting at Union Spring, where we had another convincing proof that our dear friend was qualified for the service whereunto she is called, a prophetess indeed. Accompanied by Wm. Bunting, we set out in the afternoon for Junius; crossed the Cayuga Lake on a bridge, passed by the outlet of the Seneca Lake, and through Waterloo, a handsome village and place of great business.

"27th.—Took a walk this morning to look at the country, which is handsome; good land and fine timber, but poorly watered. I met with some Friends, who gave me a description of their situation, which was poor indeed—they having fallen out some years past about building their meeting house, and the breach was not made up. It was nearly meeting time when I returned, and we went to meeting without a word being said respecting their situation. We had not sat long before our friend P. H. arose and immediately described their situation exactly, and told them more than I could have done with all that I had heard. We have frequent evidence of her being enabled to penetrate into the situation of individuals and of meetings. After this meeting we dined at the same place where we lodged, and immediately set out to attend another meeting seven miles distant, at Galena; a small-meeting, but a satisfactory one.

"30th.—In the afternoon had a meeting at South Farmington. Hard work for a time, but light sprang up, and our friend had good service among them.

"31st.—Attended Quarterly Meeting of ministers and elders at Farmington; dined and lodged at Asa Smith's.

"First of the 7th month attended Quarterly Meeting. In both of these meetings our dear friend sat in silence, and I believe I may add, in suffering.

"Second of 7th month and 5th of the week, we attended a large general meeting at this place; a pretty large house and much crowded.

The everlasting gospel was preached with Divine authority. Many hearts were tendered, and many sensible minds nearly united to our friend and her service. After a very solemn supplication this meeting concluded.

"7th mo. 8th.—Had a meeting at Orangeville, to be remembered by many. Our dear friend P. H. was led, in a very remarkable manner, to point out two states; one that had so far deviated as to doubt the immortality of the soul. This individual was spoken to in a very close and feeling manner indeed; and invited to look over the past days, and consider the feeling in younger life. The other, an individual who was called upon, in a very pecculiar manner, to prepare for another state of existence, which change was stated to be very near at hand. The warning was given in such a clear and powerful manner, that it seemed as if the whole assembly was shaken and led into close examination. It was indeed a solemn time. She supplicated in a very feeling manner, but in a most affecting and extraordinary way was she drawn forth to petition for the one whose system was shortly to float in the elements. Such seasons as this I have seldom experienced. The people separated in a very solemn manner.

"11th.—Got another horse, and went 16 miles to Somerset, on Lake Ontario, through woods and swamps. The only woman's saddle in the place was furnished for Priscilla Hunt. R. Johnson rode on a man's saddle, and I with a blind halter. Our rigging created some sport for us, but we got along safely. Had a meeting at 3 o'clock; though the company was not large, it was a precious opportunity. I may say that these women exceed any thing I have any knowledge of; they rode over bridges and causeways, where there were holes so large that if the horses had made a mis-step they would have gone in up to their bodies, and consequently thrown their riders. Here they rode with as much composure as though they were sitting in a house.

"12th of the month and 1st of the week.—We attended Heartland meeting; a mixed multitude, as is generally the case. Our dear friend had much to do among them in opening the doctrines of the Gospel, being afresh qualified therefor.

"14th.—Had a meeting at Stockport, a very busy, noisy place; abundance of Irishmen blowing rocks, and such a scene of business, I never saw, yet we had a crowded and very solemn meeting; the people of different denominations sat very quietly, while our dear friend was livingly engaged on the subject of woman's preaching, water baptism and the ordinances; all of which she opened in so clear and powerful a manner that the audience was all attention, and it seemed as if every one said amen. After this followed the subject of hireling ministry and bartering the Gospel. Such power attended, that all seemed borne down before it, and I said in my heart, what more can be said to open the eyes of the people. In some places individuals have been so powerfully spoken to in meeting, that on taking leave of her they have even cried out, and in their way poured out blessings upon the Author of good for sending such a powerful instrument among them.

"15th.—Travelled through Buffalo and through the Indian settlement to Hamburg, a handsome town. Here our dear friend P. H. was taken unwell. Next morning, the 16th, she appeared to be very much amiss. I doubted her being able to attend the meeting, as she could not sit up nor take any nourishment; but as meeting time drew nigh, (considering large notice had been given,) she concluded if we would get the carriage she would try and go, and if she could not remain she would motion to me, and I might inform the meeting, and she would return. We had not sat long before she arose and expressed a few sentences, which were accompanied with a power that produced great solemnity over the meeting. She paused a short time and rose again, being eminently clothed with the power of the Gospel. It was considered by many to be the most angelic and clear communication they had ever heard: After which she appeared in supplication in a powerful and heart-tendering manner. An ancient elder mentioned to me before we left our seats, that he believed he had never before sat in such a meeting. Indeed it was solemn and heavenly. It seemed as if all present deeply felt it. As soon as the meeting closed she was taken ill; we hurried back, got her to bed, and called in a physician. In the afternoon we moved her three miles to Elisha Baker's; he and his wife, were very kind. Our dear friend bore this and her sickness throughout, with all the patience and composure that could be expected from a humble, devoted Christian. Her disorder was very distressing, but through all, when the pain would subside a little, she was so cheerful and pleasant that it was a pleasure to be with her and wait upon her.

"19th.—Our beloved friend continued very unwell. Rachel staid with her, and I went to meeting.

"21st.—In the afternoon P. H. was so much recovered that we went on.

"8th mo. 3d and First of the week, we attended the meeting at Nerwick; a large and crowded meeting; four Methodist ministers and nearly their whole congregations attended. Two of these ministers were strangers in the place, being travelling preachers of very considerable note. They had met at the Methodist meeting house that morning, with the expectation of holding a meeting agreeably with their appointment about two miles off, but by some means heard of our meeting, and having heard previously of our Indiana Friend, a consultation took place which ended with this conclusion; to adjourn till 3 o'clock in the afternoon, and all hands go to Quaker meeting. They came in very late, but were quiet and attentive, especially the ministers. They, the two strangers, were seated facing our gallery. After meeting they came up to us, and spoke to us in such a manner as evinced their affection and great satisfaction. This meeting held till 2 o'clock and their meeting was to be at 3, but notwithstanding its length, it was quiet and solemn. The Gospel was preached with power and authority. Some particular states were pointed out in a very peculiar manner. It was a precious meeting. Many Gospel truths were clearly and livingly opened to that large assemblage of people: after which our dear friend appeared in a feeling and heart-tendering supplication. O! saith my spirit, that this labor may not be lost, but that many minds may be strengthened and encouraged, and the Lord, the helper of his own, be praised. Our beloved friend appears to be fitted for any service to which she is called, either in great meetings or small.

"5th.—Set out for Yarmouth. This day exceeded any thing: the musquitoes seemed as if they would devour us, and the roads were intolerable with mud and stumps. This being a new road through the woods, there was no place to turn out. The musquitoes were so troublesome that the women had full employ, with each of them a bush, to keep those creatures off me and themselves; with all their exertion, our faces had the appearance next day of chicken-pox. My time was taken up with minding the horses, though sometimes I had to drop the lines and fend off. We had not gone very far before our horses mired in a very deep mud hole, the wheel struck a root, and we were now planted in the mud, and these living creatures playing away upon us and our horses. We had two friends with us, one on horseback the other on foot;—the latter sprang into the mud nearly to his waist, and released the horses from the carriage; they were just able to extricate themselves. We then made a kind of bridge to get the women out to the side of a tree; after which, with ropes we fastened the horses to the end of the tongue; the friend, who was already covered with mud, put his shoulders to the wheel, and I, getting on one of the horses, with much ado we got the wagon out, and went on about half a mile; stopped at a cabin and dried our clothes and went on; arrived at Falbut Street that evening.

"6th.—Left for Yarmouth, 16 miles through the woods. Being informed that it was impossible to get there with our carriage, the neighborhood was searched for saddles and bridles: not a woman's saddle could be found. At length we were furnished with one horse, three men's saddles, (so old that we should think in our country they had done their duty,) then some kind of bridles, with which we made shift, and landed safely after crossing fields, over fences and ditches,—sometimes no road at all,—sometimes just a horse-path, over trees that had fallen across the road. Sometimes we were forced to lay down on our saddles to avoid the timber,—at other times to hold fast by the mane of the horse to keep from falling off.

"7th.—Had a meeting at Yarmouth to good satisfaction, and returned to Falbut Street.

"11th.—Set out for Yonge Street, about 90 miles. No Friends on the road, we were obliged to take tavern fare; a long, lonesome road, a great part of the way through the woods. We stopped a number of times to pick whortleberries, and our friend Priscilla entertained us some of the time with very interesting poetry. Their company and conversation being very agreeable, the time passed pleasantly through this lonely wilderness. Dined and lodged at a tavern.

"12th.—Went on to York; halted there some time; passed on and again lodged at a tavern.

"13th.—Arrived at Yonge Street.

"14th of 8th month and 5th of the week, we attended Yonge St. Monthly Meeting. Notice having been spread, a large collection of different denominations assembled, among whom our dear friend was largely opened in the spring of the Gospel; many subjects clearly explained; some pretty close work after meeting; dined and lodged at the same place; had much company to dine with us and spend the afternoon.

"19th.—Had a meeting at Pickering, where our beloved friend P. H. was enabled, in a lively and powerful manner, to sound an alarm among them; the everlasting Gospel was preached. Some things pointed out in a very remarkable manner, being a highly favored time, after several days of deep trial and heavy wading, wherein she seemed to take but little satisfaction in any thing around her. Dined at Nicholas Brown's.

"20th.—Set out for Cold Creek, a distance of 60 miles, accompanied by Ira Brown, brother to Nicholas. This day we had a pleasant ride through a wilderness country; a day of pleasantness rather more than common. We made out 50 miles. It was late at night when we arrived at our destined port. The people were gone to bed, but soon got up and set us supper. The friend's name was Freeman Clarke.

"21st.—Travelled many miles by the side of Lake Ontario. The last ten miles of this day's journey rather exceeded for dangerous roads any thing that I have seen. 2 o'clock.—Had a meeting in a barn near Lake Ontario; a large collection. Although I had been in a tried state of mind, and much unwell as to bodily health for nearly 24 hours past, yet in this meeting I was much recruited, it being a memorable time, and our dear friend much favored, and enabled to speak to the situation of many, especially to one individual, who had been much opposed to woman's preaching. A solemn and powerful supplication near the close of the meeting, produced a very great solemnity. After this good meeting, dined at a Friend's, where came a gaily dressed person, and informed us that he was the man addressed in the meeting on the subject of woman's preaching, he having been greatly opposed thereto, believing they had no right nor authority to officiate in that way. He said he had made use of the very arguments, yea, the very words she had mentioned in the meeting, and he had felt most easy to call and inform us that he was now satisfied he was mistaken, and that she was qualified and rightly commissioned to preach the Gospel.

"24th.—Had a meeting at Adolphus: the latter part of this meeting was a memorable time; our dear friend's appearance among them was attended with so much power, so full and so affecting, that the people appeared unwilling to leave the house. One individual was so tendered by being particularly spoken to, as to be brought to trembling and shedding abundance of tears. In her supplication she implored Divine goodness for our preservation in a most powerful manner, seldom, perhaps, if ever exceeded; her soul being poured forth to the sovereign Lord, the God of heaven, for the preservation of our little band, that they might be kept from harm, and enabled to move on under Divine appointment. It was a melting, heavenly time.

"26th.—Attended a meeting at First Town. Our beloved friend had acceptable service; spoke very particularly to an individual who denied the immortality of the soul. In her supplication she appeared very fervent on behalf of that individual, that his eyes might be opened to see things clearly as they were. After this meeting, went on to Kingston, a considerable town, got our carriage mended, and lodged at a tavern.

"27th.—Travelled 45 miles, through a poor and rather desolate country; lodged at a house of entertainment.

"28th.—About 3 o'clock we arrived at Leeds.

"First-day, the 29th, attended their meeting. It was held in a barn. Much might be said of this meeting, but suffice it to say, the Gospel was preached with Divine authority, after which our dear friend appeared in a powerful supplication. She then opened the subject of women's preaching, which was handled in a masterly manner, to the great satisfaction of many present. She then bade them an affectionate farewell; after which she appeared again in a solemn supplication. Thus ended the last meeting in Canada.

"Eighth month 29th.—Left for Brachville, sixteen miles—lodged at a tavern. Early next morning we went down to the ferry, and got our carriage on board, but this great river, the St. Lawrence, being so moved with the wind in the night, and a fresh gale in the morning, that the ferrymen refused to go, and we were obliged to take out our carriage and return to the tavern. Took breakfast,—waited then till noon and dined, and about 5 o'clock set out in earnest, but a number of villagers followed us to the side of the water, and persisted in saying it would not do to venture, confidently asserting that the boat would fill before we got half over. A person who was in the boat for the purpose of crossing, took the alarm, and stepped out just as we were about to set off. In the midst of this clamor and confusion, our friend, P. H., spoke in an audible voice and said: "We have been detained too long already. There is no danger; we shall land safely." We set off immediately. Soon the wind ceased,—a perfect calm ensued, and the water, that just before appeared dangerous, now became still, and a very pleasant ride we had over that great river. The ferrymen noticed it as something remarkable. Lodged at a tavern on the York side.

"31st.—Travelled about forty-five miles; some very bad roads; arrived at John Strickland's about dusk, and lodged there.

"Ninth month 2d.—Had a meeting at Indian River; a number of other societies attended.

Hard work in the fore part, but ended well,—some things were opened perhaps in a clearer light than many of them had before heard. A good meeting. Dined at John Strickland's, Jr.—went on to Leray.

"3d.—Had a meeting there—a mixed company. The subject of Baptism was treated on with such clearness that no room was left for gainsaying.

"Ninth month 7th.—Had a meeting at Lee in the morning, and one in the afternoon at Western; both these meetings were somewhat remarkable. An unusual degree of solemnity prevailed. Individual states were impressively addressed. Priscilla said there was one present who was not a member of our Religious Society. He had been engaged in preaching the Gospel, though his labors had not been received by all, but if he was faithful, he would be enabled to sound the trumpet with more clearness and power, and his accusers, or those that had persecuted him, would come and acknowledge they were wrong and he was right. It was a memorable time; after which, a minister among those called Christians arose. His heart seemed full. He spoke a few minutes impressively. I thought it tended to increase the solemnity of the meeting. He appeared very candid and sincere. Our dear friend P. H. being eminently clothed with the spirit of supplication, the meeting closed in a very comfortable manner.

"8th.—This afternoon had a meeting in a school-house, where our beloved Friend had hard work. She said it was trying to find that her love to them was not reciprocated. She had come a great way in the love of the Gospel to visit them, having no other view than the good of their souls, and the peace of her own mind. She moved on, carefully, steadily watching the stepping stones, and was led to speak in a very remarkable and personal manner. She turned towards an individual and told him that if he did not repent, turn about, humble himself, and amend his ways, he would be so left to himself, that an ignominious prison would be his portion. The company was small, and the circumstances such that her service must rest upon one out of two or three. She was, I think, sensible who-it was, and I thought it not difficult for me to determine. A solemn supplication ended this meeting.

"9th.—Went on to Westmoreland, attended a meeting appointed at 10 o'clock, where we sat long in silence; every thing seemed cold and uncomfortable. I thought there was nothing to be done, and so I closed the meeting, and was walking out, when I heard some person speaking. I looked round, and saw P. H. on her feet. I again took my seat; she told them she was sensible they had been negligent in notifying their neighbors of this meeting; that she had come far to see them, but through their neglect she must now leave the neighborhood in pain. Some of them were much troubled, being sensible the charge was true. After meeting several expressed that the like cause of complaint should not occur again while they resided in the neighborhood. P. H. mentioned to me that she had looked round at me to close the meeting, for she felt nothing to do there, but while the people were rising, it opened upon her mind to leave a few hints of that kind, which, I expect, will be long remembered by some of them. It was a satisfaction to find that I had not closed the meeting too soon.

"Bridgewater, 11th.—Had a meeting here

very much made up of other societies,—a favored time. The Gospel was preached with great clearness. A free ministry was treated on, and the entire insufficiency of human abilities, though aided by theological study, to confer the power to preach, was clearly shown. An impressive caution was also given, not to attempt to preach the Gospel without being taught and empowered by the Great Head of the church. A young man was present, who had entered or was on the point of entering upon the study of divinity. He was so affected and reached by the communication, that it was thought by some who afterwards heard him converse on the subject, that he would undoubtedly give up his pursuit. He said he had never before heard any thing upon the subject which affected him so powerfully.

"12.—Had a meeting at Madson, in which our dear friend was enlarged in Gospel authority, and enabled to set forth with convincing clearness and power many subjects of vital importance, closing her communication by a most impressive description of the New Jersualem, or state of the redeemed. When she sat down, a solemn silence continued over the meeting, when a person, not a member with Friends, from the far end of the house, arose and fully united with what had been said, recapitulating some of the subjects which had been mentioned, and begging those present to treasure them up, and endeavor to profit by them. The solemnity of the meeting was not disturbed, and under this covering P. H. fervently supplicated for our preservation and the enlargement of the Messiah's kingdom. This blessed meeting held long, yet the people did not seem willing to leave the house, those in the gallery having to move first. I consider we have had many and abundant evidences of the divine authority of the mission of our Friend.

"13.—Attended a meeting appointed at Brookfield; a number of different denominations collected. This meeting continued long in silence, but light and life at length arising, our dear friend arose therewith, and was enabled to clear herself. Many things of deep interest were opened in the life and clearly explained, I believe, to the satisfaction of that mixed multitude; a short but very lively and powerful supplication closed the meeting, which, I believe, was a good one.

"16th.—Had a meeting at Smyrna, mostly of other societies, which was a heavenly season; many truths were illustrated in a manner, I believe, exceeding any thing of the kind that I have ever heard in clearness, power and authority. The audience was very attentive. Water baptism was shown to be a Jewish rite, and the people were called to that spiritual baptism, which immerses souls in the stream of love and life. After a short and solemn pause, she appeared in an angelic supplication.

"We went on towards Burlington. On our way we were overtaken with a most tremendous storm. It was truly awful. The clouds, which were of an uncommon color, came over us very fast, producing almost midnight darkness. The lightening flew round our carriage like balls of fire, and the thunder seemed to shake the earth. We reached a tavern shed, just as it began to rain, and it was the most favorable place we could have found for several miles. The storm came on so rapidly that we were obliged to stay in the carriage. The rain fell in such torrents, that in a very few minutes a sufficient quantity of water to turn a mill came rushing under the shed. It seemed as if all would be washed away, the wind blew terrifically, and it very soon commenced hailing. The hail stones broke all the windows, except one, of the large tavern house. In the house all was afloat, so that we fared better in our carriage than if we had been in it. P. H. sat in the carriage viewing the tremendous and awful scene with entire composure and serenity. We were within two miles of the place where we expected to remain for the night. After the storm had abated; we went on, but found, had we reached there before, we should, in all probability, have fared worse than we did, the house being more elevated, and consequently more exposed to the fury of the storm. The friend came out to receive us, and told us they would have been very glad of our company, but the house was in such a condition, the windows broken, and the floors all afloat, that they had not a dry bed, and they doubted their being able to accommodate us with any degree of comfort. We passed on some distance, and lodged at a tavern; though the windows here were much broken, and part of the house in a poor plight, yet we were comfortably accommodated.

"17th.—This morning we set out, but proceeded very slowly, for the trees were so blown across the road, that our pilot was obliged to get the supervisors and several hands to cut a road through, while we sat in the carriage. As they cleared away, we moved on a short distance, and stopped again for them to clear away further; and so we went on. We got through to our lodging place.

"18th.—Had a meeting at Burlington; some close and plain work here. Many hearts were tendered, and some nearly united with our beloved friend and her labors of love among them.

"Ninth month 19th.—We attended a large and crowded meeting at Butternutts, general notice having been given. Some time previous to our arrival, a newspaper had circulated through the village and neighborhood some account of our dear friend's meeting and communication at Merion, in Montgomery County, Pennsylvania, which created a great anxiety in the minds of the people of different denominations to see and hear her. In the early part of this meeting, it being a large house and very crowded, some boys appeared to be much unsettled. They were spoken to on the subject, which seemed to have a good effect; they settled down at length and all became quiet. A solemn covering spread over the meeting, under which P. H. arose, being eminently clothed with power from on high. Her clear and cogent reasoning, her matter and manner, her language and strength of utterance, I believe exceeded the most sanguine expectations raised by the account they had received. Perhaps I should not say amiss if I set it down as the greatest display of oratory that I ever heard flow from human lips. Several of the latter meetings have been extraordinary seasons, but I think, for beautiful language, clearness and strength of utterance, this has exceeded them all.

"20th.—Had a meeting here in a schoolhouse; though small, yet a comfortable one. Dined at a tavern on the way, no Friend's house being near, and the distance to next meeting not admitting our going back over the hills. Had a very rough ride along a branch of the Susquehanna.

"21st.—Had a meeting at Unadilla. Some close work with individuals who made a high profession, but the gospel flowed freely to the poor in spirit. It was an instructive meeting to many.

"22d.—Had a large, crowded meeting at Laurens, in which our beloved friend was very lively in communication and powerful in supplication. It appears very evident she is qualified for the arduous task in which she has embarked, and fitted for every service.

"23d.—Set out for Harpersfield, a distance of twenty miles; the roads were thought too bad for our carriage, and so N. N. took us in his open wagon. We arrived there in the afternoon; and that evening, by candle-light, we had a highly favored meeting. A few Friends, but mostly other societies. Some acknowledged they were well paid for coming; others said they could have been content to have stayed till day-light. The Gospel flowed freely among them, and the meeting ended with a heart-tendering supplication.

"25th.—This morning our dear friend did not feel easy to leave the place without having the people collected; which was done, and I being absent, was informed by some that were present that it was a memorable time. From thence they proceeded on to Middlefield, I having returned with N. N. to Laurey, where we had left our horses and carriage.

"30th.—Attended their meeting at Duansburg. P. H. was clear and powerful in communication and supplication. A comfortable and instructive meeting.

"Tenth month 2d, and first of the week we were at Renselaerville meeting. It was large, and the fore part was dull, but light sprung up and truth prevailed. Our beloved friend had excellent service among them; some deep mysteries were unfolded, and evidences furnished that we were not left, but that He who laid a concern upon our dear friend, was still with her, giving ability to perform every required duty.

"Tenth mo. 3d.—Left for Middleburg. Had a meeting at this place. Our dear friend expressed her travail and desire for the people, that they might come to the inward Teacher, who stood prepared to teach all who were willing to be taught of Him. An instructive meeting.

"4th.—Attended a meeting appointed at Oakhill; a very extraordinary time. The Gospel was preached with power, and was expressed pure and without mixture. Our dear friend was surely eminently favored. We were solemnized, and I believe could have said amen to her supplication. After meeting went on to Coeymans.

"5th.—Attended meeting at that place. P. H. sat the meeting through in silence. She evidently felt that something was wrong. After meeting we found that notice had not been given to others, and but little among Friends, it being their usual meeting day, for which neglect she felt easy to leave the meeting in silence, and let it rest upon the neglectful or lukewarm.

"6th.—Attended a meeting at New Baltimore. Some time before, in the neighborhood, a report was circulated that P. H. was preaching the Baptists' doctrine, and promulgating their principles. A man who had been disowned from our Society, and was now a minister of another, had said he would go forty miles to hear her, and if she did not preach such doctrines as he approved, he would openly oppose her in the meeting. All this was told me the evening before the meeting; several Friends having convened at our lodging, were desirous of having our friend P. H. informed of what was reported. I urged the impropriety of such a measure, and informed them that I believed she would be furnished with knowledge and strength for the occasion, be that what it might. After considerable more being said on both sides, it was concluded to say nothing to her about it, and not a word of it was imparted to her.

"7th.—Went to meeting. After sitting some time in silence, our exercised sister rose on the subject of baptism, being eminently qualified to do it justice. She cleared up all the disputed points in a remarkable manner. It was a highly favored time. The communication and supplication were attended with that power that chains all down that stands opposed. After meeting, a Friend expressed satisfaction that, without any outward knowledge of the facts, she was so peculiarly led and enabled completely to clear up the matter. It was a great relief to concerned Friends; they thinking it would have a salutary effect on the neighborhood.

"9th.—We had an evening meeting, which was large and remarkably favored; the Gospel stream ran high. Many subjects were opened and treated on with great clearness and authority. A profound silence spread over the meeting, and our dear friend was eminently clothed with the spirit of supplication. It was a remarkable time to me, and I believe to many others. It was mentioned by some as being a most heavenly meeting. Next day, being 1st of the week and 10th of the month, we attended Ghent meeting; a large concourse of people. Hard work in the fore part; some opposition felt, but Truth gained the victory, and all opposition seemed to be removed.

"4th of the week and 13th of the month we attended a meeting at Troy; notice having been given, a considerable collection of people assembled. We sat long in silence. At length P. H. arose and said: "Because thou art neither cold nor hot, I will spew thee out of my mouth," and then took her seat. But before the meeting closed, she delivered a short and close testimony calculated to impress the hearers.

"14th.—Set out for East Hoosack or Adams. This day I suppose we were in both Vermont and Massachusetts States; travelled a distance of forty-five miles. Next day had a comfortable meeting, and returned part way back. Lodged at a tavern. In the night it began to snow, and continued nearly all day; we travelled ten miles in the storm.

"15th.—Had a meeting at Pittstown; a precious, good meeting. Our beloved friend was enabled to preach the Gospel with life and power, and was much favored in supplication. Many hearts were tenderly affected in these meetings. John Lawton, a Friend from Athens, met us here with a prospect of taking my place, and I am about to be released to return home. It is a close trial to me to part with those with whom I have travelled nearly six months in sweet union, they being very near to me. I had been out longer than I expected, and as I could now resign my charge to a suitable Friend, I felt it was the right time for me to return to my family. Some time previous to our arriving in this neighborhood, I had spoken to some of our friends of my prospect of leaving, desiring the service might fall on one fitted for it. John Lawton was mentioned, without knowing that it would suit him to leave home. When we came to his house and the subject was opened to him, he informed us that agreeably to his secret impressions, he had been preparing to leave home, apprehending it would be his duty to accompany some Friend on a religious visit, but who it might be, or where he would go, he knew not, until we came into the place. He was ready *in a few hours* to leave his home for several months. This made it much easier for me to leave them, and the attraction to my family, from whom I had long been absent, was powerful. Next day we parted. They to pursue their northern route, and I for home. I reached home on Fourth-day, the 19th of 10th month, 1823, and found my family enjoying usual health, for which, and other favors, I felt very thankful.

"Upon a retrospective view of this journey, and the different scenes we have passed through, I have seen, in some instances, where I have fallen short of my duty, and perhaps in many where I have not done as well as I might have done, but through all I can now say, I feel a satisfaction in having given up to what I believed was required of me, being furnished from time to time with sufficient evidence of its being right. Some trials were permitted to assail me, which, perhaps, might have been avoided if I had more closely attended to my proper business; but He who weighs the mountains in scales, and the hills in a balance, sees not as man seeth, but looketh at the heart, and judgeth of the motive; and happy for us that we have such a judge, who judges not as man, but righteously. I have seen the hand of Providence in many instances. Sometimes in opening a way where there appeared to be no way; helping through difficulties that otherwise would have been insurmountable. In and through all we have abundant cause to thank God and take courage. We have had some close trials to pass through, and some pleasant scenes, and some truly edifying and instructive seasons. Some passages of Scripture have been more clearly explained than I have before heard, and views given on different subjects that were new and interesting. The closing of many of the meetings under a clear and powerful supplication has been very solemn and affecting: many marks of unity and sympathy with our dear friend and her labors have been evinced, not only by the members of our Society, but abundantly among others, and my mind has again and again been furnished with evidence to satisfy me under what authority she was moving, so that the language of my heart then was, and still is, to her, as a humble, devoted handmaid of the Lord, "go on and prosper." May the God of Heaven be with and go before her, making way through all opposition, so that through her as an instrument in His hand, qualified and anointed for the service, sons may be gathered from afar, and daughters from the ends of the earth. I wish not to exceed the proper bounds, but to ascribe the praise where she herself would place it, to Him who alone can qualify for such service. Yet those who are truly devoted, who travel far and wide, and are willing to spend and be spent for the good of others, are entitled to our sympathy, and demand our respect, and agreeably to the apostle's sentiment, are worthy of double honor.

"I have many times thought it was a favor that Priscilla was so agreeably furnished with a companion from her own Quarterly Meeting. They appear to travel in great unity and harmony, and my desire is that it may continue, and that on their return to their families and friends, they may each experience that reward, which is the result of continuing faithful to the end."

Although James Walton had travelled for six months in close unity and sympathy with these Friends, he was not without many discouragements, and doubts would sometimes arise as to the propriety of so long a separation from his family. On one occasion these doubts pressed so heavily upon him that, for several days, his secret conclusion was, that if Priscilla should tell him she was released from further service, he would willingly wait upon her all the way to her home in Indiana, if by that means he might be at liberty to return to his own home.

These feelings he kept to himself; but one morning as they rode along, they came to a fork in the road where there was a finger board, one finger of which pointed to the West, toward her home, and the other towards the place where her next meeting was to be held. As they neared this point, Priscilla laid her hand upon his shoulder and said, "Stop, James." He drew in the reins, and they halted: after a few moments of solemn quiet, she said, "Now, James, thou art to decide which road we take." The evidence thus furnished, that she had been drawn into secret sympathy with his unexpressed feelings, and had shared a burden which he thought he was bearing alone, was a confirmation to his troubled mind, that it would be right for him to proceed, and he cheerfully took the road which led them into further service.

Some further account of Priscilla's religious services during this visit have been furnished by a Friend then residing in the State of New York, which we give in her own language:

"In the summer of 1823, Priscilla Hunt visited all the meetings of Friends in Scipio Quarterly Meeting, several of which I attended. I was deeply impressed with her sweetness of spirit and deep indwelling. Her communications were wonderfully adapted to the state of the meetings she attended, and individuals were frequently addressed publicly, and their characteristics described so minutely as to leave no doubt to whom her remarks applied. At one meeting she was very prophetic, saying that the time was not far distant when the meeting would go down, through the creaturely activity of one individual, adding, 'Dear brother, thou hast done much harm; thou hast drawn thy sword in defence of the Truth and ran, saying the Lord has sent thee, when He has not. The Truth has no need of thee to defend it, but if thou will come to the Truth, *it will defend thee.* When thou art gone the meeting will be re-established, and will increase in numbers.' This prediction has been strictly fulfilled. It was truly a memorable and deeply affecting time. The solemn rebukes and affectionate warnings were so humbly, and faithfully, and needfully given, that some were comforted, many were alarmed, and others awakened to inquire and wonder."

An extract of a sermon delivered by P. H. in one of the New England cities in 1824, is worthy of record in this connection, as containing a prophecy, which has since been literally fulfilled:

"The zeal of thine house hath eaten me up." Where are the wise men? Where are the counsellors of Israel? Are they on the house-top, or have they fled to the mountains? Call home my people, saith the Lord. They have departed from my councils; they have risen in judgment against one another. They have forsaken the living God; have hewn unto themselves broken cisterns, that can hold no water. There has been a departure in those who stood at the helm of government. Had truth been at the helm, you would not now be in your present state of confusion. You have gone forth in your own strength to do the work of the Lord; you have run before your guide. You have called Lord, Lord, when you had no command; you have asumed the seat of judgment in your own wills; you have suffered wrath and fierce contention to arise among you; you have poured out boiling water on the heads of the brethren, and called it the waters of life. My soul is bowed down within me, and woe is me if I deliver not this message; the voice of it to my mind is as children pouring boiling water upon one another's heads, and each dipping from the same fountain. For want of true judgment my people lay slain on the right and on the left, and if you cease not to act in this spirit, the people will be scattered, till not one shall be left in the meeting of the name of Friend."

She then went on to describe the state of the meeting, and said:

"You have looked at one another till your own image was reflected as in the vapor, and the evil which is in yourselves you have attributed to a brother. If we only rightly examine ourselves, what appears like a mountain in another, will be little more than a mole hill. The door of mercy is still open, and the language is this day, come home, come home, and you shall be favored again to drink of the living stream which will quench the spirit of contention within you. Until self is cast out, the pure spirit of truth cannot reign. It is self that strives to have the ascendency, and wishes to be thought great, while the true follower of God is humble, esteeming himself as the least and as a servant. When man sees his heart as it really is, and this the light of truth will show him, he finds enough to do there, without condemning a brother. If a man be wise, he will be careful to have the beam removed out of his own eye before he attempts to cast the mote out of his brother's; for, while he is in error, he cannot point out the right way to others. Therefore I entreat you, beloveds, to take this home into the secret chambers of your hearts; there will be room enough to apply it there. Say not it belongs to a brother, but each take it to himself. Of our blessed Lord it was said, 'in his humiliation his judgment was taken away.' When all that is of the creature is humbled, we feel no disposition to judge one another. What was the language of Jesus when he was reviled, persecuted and nailed to the cross, and this, too, by the high Priest and rulers of the people, 'Father forgive them, they know not what they do.' I believe from present impressions that there are those within the sound of my voice whose hands hang down upon their loins, whose mouths are bowed down in the dust, who are willing to be counted as nothing amongst men, if they do but stand firm in their obedience to God. To these I may say, you must be numbered with the transgressors and condemned with thieves; you must be reproached, and the finger of scorn pointed at you, and you may enter into a state comparable to that of being entombed, or as dead, and your usefulness among men may appear to be at an end. But the ministering angel will appear, and the stone will be rolled away from the mouth of the sepulchre, and you shall rise in glory and sit at the right hand in the kingdom.

"But it appears to me that the number of these is very small. I know nothing of you but from my feelings. I am a stranger in a strange land, and I have often to feel that I am alone and among a strange people. I feel sensible that I am rejected by some among you, and those, too, of high profession; but I am delivered from the fear of man, and in the love of God my heart salutes you all. I know that I love you, and I know that I love God, and in that feeling I can rest unmoved. The frowns and scoffs of men, their flattery and their praise, are all nothing to the soul that is united and centered in God, that depends upon Him alone. But I entreat you, beloveds, for your own sakes, not to despise the message this day delivered to you, however weak the instrument, for those that despise the least servant of God, despise Him. They that reject the message, reject Him that sent it: the truly wise are alone ready to be instructed. The least among us may be made useful; we may learn wisdom from the mouth of a child; but the poor man who is unwilling to receive what is sent him, and always gives to others what was designed for himself, must ever remain poor."

After her return from this visit, she formed a second marriage connection.

In alluding to this chapter in her history, we feel a tender caution towards all concerned, and desire to withdraw no further than is absolutely necessary the mantle which time has thrown over the painful circumstances connected with her second marriage, by which her name became Priscilla Cadwallader.

There cannot be a doubt that our dear friend was fully impressed with the importance of humbly seeking divine counsel in a proceeding which has such an important and lasting influence, for good or ill, as that of choosing a companion for life, and we know that this counsel was not withheld from her on this occasion; but in a moment of weakness, as she herself acknowledged, she allowed the persuasions of others to prevail over the clear sense of right with which she was favored, and took a step that brought upon her years of sorrow and suffering. These trials she bore with Christian meekness, their seeming effect being to deepen and refine; and she quietly and uncomplainingly pursued the path of duty, leaving her cause to Him who knows the secret of every heart, and who, in his unfailing mercy, withdraws not his life-giving power from the contrite spirit, because of one act of disobedience. Under the humbling influence of this Power, she was enabled eminently to manifest that her daily dependence was on Him, who could not only redeem from weakness, but renewedly qualify for the work to which she was appointed, and she subsequently gave abundant evidence, through the deeply baptizing character of her ministry, and the solemnity attending her supplications, that she experienced near access to the ever-living Presence, the alone qualifying Power.

The record of this mis-step of our beloved friend, may teach us, that gifted and chosen instruments do not always furnish models for our example, and that our only safety is in reliance upon the inward Director, and obedience to its monitions.

In the year 1829 our friend, Priscilla Cadwallader, opened a concern in her Monthly Meeting as expressed in the following certificate :

"Our esteemed friend, P. Cadwallader, in a weighty manner, opened in this meeting a concern that had rested upon her mind for some time, to pay a visit in Gospel love to the inhabitants of North America and some of the West India islands, as truth may open the way. After a time of weighty deliberation thereon, this meeting fully unites therewith, and she is left at liberty to pursue her prospect as best wisdom may direct, she being a minister in good esteem among Friends, and as such we recommend her to all people to whom these may come, with a desire that she may be enabled to return to her family and friends with the answer of peace to her own mind. Signed by direction of

Blue River Monthly Meeting, held in Washington County, Indiana, the 4th of 7th mo., 1829.

MICHAEL NEWBY, } Clerks."
MARY D. NEWBY, }

We believe this was her first visit east of the mountains after the separation, which took place among Friends in 1827.

Some of the causes which produced this event were seen and publicly alluded to by Priscilla Cadwallader, (then Hunt,) several years before it took place. Her mind was introduced into deep exercise on this account, and in the openings of Truth she felt it right to remain in religious connection with those, who she believed were concerned to maintain the original ground upon which our religious Society was established.

In the prosecution of the service alluded to, she was engaged about seven years.

As she travelled from place to place her society was again much sought, and large gatherings would assemble wherever she rested from the labor of the day. The following incidents furnished by M. H. C. show her simplicity of character and general watchfulness, and that she was not drawn into expression, either in public meetings or in private circles, merely because it appeared to be expected of her.

"On one occasion at my father's house, where there was a large company collected, a dear old friend from the city, who was often with her and was looking for and desiring a religious opportunity, soon had the company all quiet. After sitting a long time in silence, Priscilla calmly observed, that 'it was an important lesson which every Christian should learn, to be silent when commanded,' and the opportunity closed."

The same Friend says:

"I attended a meeting appointed for her several miles distant. We sat, perhaps, an hour in silence, when she arose with these words: 'What meaneth this, that there is no preaching to-day?' A young man of our company remarked after meeting, that she uttered the exact language that was passing through his mind at the time.'

Among the items concerning this visit, which we have been able to obtain, is an extract of a sermon, delivered at Friends' meeting, Darby, Pa., 7th mo. 21st, 1831.

"What shall I do unto thee? O Ephraim; O Judah, what shall I do unto thee, for your goodness is as the morning cloud and as the early dew that passes away.' Therefore get thee into thy tent, and dwell in it, lest that which has been so abundantly handed forth shall be entirely withdrawn." This language was sounded in my ears soon after I took my seat among you. 'What shall I do unto thee, O, Ephraim; what shall I do unto thee, O Judah; for I hear your goodness is as the morning cloud and the early dew, that passes away.' I was willing to take it to myself, conceal it in my own breast and improve upon it. But finding it is not for me alone, I feel a woe if I warn not this people, and take not warning myself. Therefore, my beloved friends, let us gather home; let us dwell in our tent, and that is God. And there is no other tent in which the mind of man can safely dwell. And I believe there never was a day nor a time when there was more need for this people to dwell in their tents—for here our safety assuredly lies. For I believe, from awful impressions as I pass through the land, there are more storms arising, greater than have yet been witnessed by this people. And those who are not founded in God, whose souls are not anchored in perfect love, will be wiped away, and carried wholly into the vortex of confusion. For behold there cometh *storms* and *tempests* and a *deluge of blood*. And I do not find that I have much more to say unto you, than to warn you to gather home to your God—for nothing else will screen you from danger, and no other arm can protect you.

"Do I not hear, in my spiritual ear—I have long heard it—the alarm of war, the loud roar of cannon, the clashing of swords, and horsemen rushing to battle? And I believe that this day is nigher at hand than many are aware of; a day of treading down, and a day of bloodshed; And it will be 'seen that every battle of the warrior is with confused noise and garments rolled in blood.' But this shall be a day, like the day of the Lord, 'that cometh with burning and fuel of fire.' And I entreat you to be willing to *come* to *this* that is '*with burning and fuel of fire,'* that it may consume all the sin and transgression of the heart, purify the soul, and bring it unto God. I can tell you, beloveds, and I do tell you in awful fear, that I have long seen, *sons* wrestling in bonds, and their bands will burst, and they will leap as tigers, from their dens, and then, wo, wo, to the inhabitants of North America. Thus I feel engaged to warn all that are now present, and to invite you to come home and centre in Him who is perfect love. And there is no other weapon that will defend you but perfect love, and you will find this to be a rock of safety; and although the deluge of blood may come, yet this will bear your souls above all. For God will preserve his children who depend upon him, and who have no other arm nor place of refuge; these he will marvellously protect and hold them in the hollow of his holy hand. And all who do experience this day of the Lord, do find the truth of this, that it comes with 'burning and fuel of fire,' and will consume all that is comparable to wood, hay or stubble; it will burn up all vain notions. And thus it is that righteousness will come unto us, and the Sun of righteousness arise with healing in his wings, as was declared by the mouth of one of the prophets; 'Behold the day cometh saith the Lord, that shall burn as an oven, and all that are proud, and all that do wickedly, shall be as stubble, and the fire of the Lord shall utterly consume them; but unto them that fear my name, shall the Sun of righteousness arise, with healing in his wings.' Now this is the reward of the righteous, and these have nothing to fear. But the sinner and transgressor must perish, fearfulness shall surprise the hypocrite, and sinners will be made afraid. This language was used formerly, and it may be used in the present day,—and the time is near at hand when it will be applicable; for 'the sinners in Zion will be made afraid, fearfulness [shall] surprise the hypocrite.' Now, 'who among us shall dwell with everlasting burnings; who among us shall dwell with the devouring fire? he that worketh righteousness, and speaketh uprightly; he that despises the gains of oppression; that shutteth his hands from the holding of bribes; that stoppeth his ears from the hearing of blood; and shutteth his eyes from seeing evil—his place of defence shall be the munition of rocks—his bread shall be given him, his water shall be sure.'

" Here the righteous can dwell in safety, and be at peace with God. And blessed are they who receive him in the way of his coming, and who endure this day that consumes all that his holy will hath a controversy with; blessed are those who can, in sincerity of heart, adopt the language of Jesus Christ, 'Not my will but thine, O God, be done.' For in this blessed state, where the mind comes to dwell in perfect love, all fear is cast out, and where there is no fear there is no torment, said one of the Apostles,—and if our souls dwell in this perfect love, we have nothing to fear; for it is this that triumphs over death, hell, and the grave. It is this that makes us perfect, even as our Father who is in heaven is perfect; and though many may think this is an impossibility—and say it is impossible for man to become as perfect as God—yet there is nothing required of us but what we have ability given us to perform, and this is a divine commandment, an injunction of Jesus Christ, " Be ye therefore *perfect* even as your Father who is in heaven is perfect." And how are we to come to this. The only way that we can come to it, is to live in perfect obedience to his Divine will. And as we come to dwell in God, and God in us, we shall dwell in perfection, for God is perfect, and we shall dwell in perfection, just so far, as we live in obedience to the Father's will; and every rational soul may come and dwell in the love of God; all have power to receive his kind offers. He is a God nigh at hand—He is Omnipresent, and all who come unto him, are enlightened to walk in the paths of peace and perfection. But if we remain in darkness and ignorance, the fault is our own—for man was not designed to dwell in darkness, he was made to inherit the bright regions of eternal day, to come forth in light, and to be alive in the eternal Word. Therefore if man remains in darkness it is his own fault, and the reason is, because he transgresses the Divine law; he will not hearken to the call of God, nor open to the beloved of souls; while he stands inviting all, wooing all, calling all,—saying unto them 'open unto me.' Now here is the express invitation of his eternal love. 'Behold I stand at the door and knock, if any man will hear my voice and open unto me, I will come in and sup with him, and he with me.'"

We are informed that on the afternoon of the day in which this sermon was delivered, a Friend queried of her, " Priscilla what didst thou mean ? For what was this prophecy ?" She replied, " I cannot tell when it will be accomplished, I may not live to see it, but, whoever lives 50 years longer, will see America very different from what it now is, in regard to African Slavery."

In the spring of 1832, she made a general visit through Cape May, Cumberland and Salem Counties, also to the meetings composing Haddonfield and Burlington quarters, to the satisfaction and comfort of the visited. Many meetings were appointed in school-houses and the places of worship of other religious denominations. Some were among the colored people in their own houses. These meetings were times of great favor and enlargement. She visited many places where no Friends' meeting had previously been held, sometimes pointing out with her finger the direction to which her mind was turned, and as these pointings were attended to, small isolated settlements would be discovered and meetings held in them to edification and comfort. Several years after, intelligent persons, not members of our religious society, acknowledged to one of the Friends who accompanied her through these parts, that they were the most remarkable meetings they had ever attended, and the individuals appeared much impressed with the Truth as she declared it.

One meeting held at Shiloh, in the meeting house of the "Seventh-day Baptists" was a truly baptizing season. At the close of Priscilla's communication, the minister of the congregation, an aged man and a most excellent and practical Christian, bore testimony to the truths delivered, and commended them to the pious attention of those present.

An evidence of her ability to feel closely with those she visited, is thus narrated by one of her companions as occurring during this visit.

"The meeting we were about to attend, was

gathered when we arrived, and when I went into the meeting house, after fastening my horses, I observed that Priscilla's face was towards the men's gallery. This was so unusual, that it attracted my attention. After a time of silence she arose with a close, searching testimony, addressed to an individual. At length she said, 'I feel that I could lay my hand on thy head. Wilt thou sell thy soul, for ten dollars?' etc. etc. The silence and awe which covered the meeting may well be imagined. I was afterwards informed that Friends of that place had been exceedingly tried in consequence of a disagreement between two of their members. One believed that in paying the other a debt, he had given him in mistake two 10 dollar notes instead of one. The other said he had received *only* 10 dollars. In this way the matter stood, when Priscilla visited the meeting, and the Friend who was charged with wrong doing, sat in the place toward which her looks were directed."

We have some further particulars, taken from the letters of our late friend John Jackson, who (then in his 22d year) was one of her companions through the southern part of New Jersey.

"Cape Island, 2d. mo. 1832.

* * * * "Although there are no *Friends* in these parts, and many of the people much prejudiced against women's preaching, yet the way is remarkably opened; the mountains of opposition skip like rams and the little hills like lambs. The first place where we stopped, after we got from among Friends was at the house of a Baptist. They treated us with that respect and hospitality, which form a striking feature in the character of a Christian. We had an appointed meeting near this place in a school house, which was full to overflowing, and the people appeared to be well pleased. Several of the Baptists followed on to several of the other meetings, and when we parted with them, some of them shed many tears and expressed a wish that if we or any of our friends should come that way again, we should not pass them by.

* * * * "Sea Shore. Last evening we held the first Friends' meeting that was ever held at this place, and many of the people had never heard a woman nor a Friend preach. One of the ministers made all the opposition he could to a meeting being had; he refused to let us have his house, and told his congregation that

he had good reasons to oppose it. He said, women had no right to preach; it was contrary to Scripture, for they were expressly commanded to keep silence in the churches. Our meeting was held in one of the large boarding houses, and the people were very still and paid great attention. Although Priscilla *knew nothing* of what their minister had said against her, she was lead to offer a different view of Paul's language, and showed clearly, that in Christ male and female are one—it being the immortal soul that constitutes the man in Christ; and that to debar women from preaching the gospel, was going back to the Mahometan religion, instead of coming into the brightness of the glorious gospel day. The people appeared to be well pleased with her views and manifested great kindness toward us at the close of the meeting.

"Port Elizabeth. Friends in N. Jersey feel great interest in the extensive prospect of our friend Priscilla, and they endeavor to bear their part of the burden and thus fulfil the law of Christ. We have had meetings every day since I wrote, mostly along the sea side, and although they have been very much from among Friends, they have been interesting occasions and the people appear well satisfied. I believe Priscilla's labors in these parts will be long remembered, for impressions have been made upon the minds of many, that time nor circumstances will not be likely to erase.

"The people have been accustomed to hear spoken of from the pulpit, 'the terrors and frowns of an angry God,' and when they come to hear a gospel that speaks peace to the obedient soul,—that publishes the glad tidings of salvation, and saith unto Zion thy God reigneth—when they hear that the judgments of Heaven are not sent in anger—when they hear the dark doctrine of election and reprobation overturned by Scripture testimony, and the terms of salvation set before them in language that they can comprehend—when they find the strong walls of prejudice which have existed in their minds against women's preaching broken down—when they find that Priscilla covets not the money nor the applause of men, but has at heart the present and future well-being of her fellow heirs to a never-ending eternity—they cannot but give her the right hand of fellowship and wish her God speed. One man and his wife (Methodists by profession) followed us to six meetings in Cape

May County; they appeared well satisfied and the man told me at the last meeting, that he had heard much about Priscilla, and wished to hear and judge for himself; that now he was satisfied and could give a favorable report to others.

"At Cape May we had an appointed meeting in a house that was built for the accommodation of all societies. There were many Methodists, Baptists, some Presbyterians and a few Friends in attendance. Priscilla commenced with the language of Scripture, 'Come brother, come sister, let us go up to the mountain of the Lord, to the house of the God of Jacob; He will teach us of his ways and we will walk in his paths; then shall we know the law to go forth out of Zion and the word of the Lord out of Jerusalem." Many very interesting subjects, connected with the happiness of man, were brought into view, his fall—his restoration and redemption, etc. Toward the close she remarked, 'There is not one among you who loves his native home better than I do, and if I could remain there in the love of God, I would not be seen travelling among you; but when I hear the language 'all souls are mine,'—when I hear the command to go forth and proclaim the glad tidings of the gospel of my Lord and master, my greatest peace consists in obedience to his command, and I find the truth of what the blessed Master declared, 'In this world ye shall have tribulation but in me ye shall have peace.' In that love which desires your present and eternal welfare, I bid you farewell; and remember the way to farewell, is to do well. Live in love with one another, and the God of love and peace will be with you —and that you may be happy in time and through all eternity, is the desire of your tribulated sister."

"Cedarville, 3mo., 1832.—On First-day afternoon we had a large meeting in a Baptist meeting house. Priscilla rose with this language, 'Behold mine elect, whom I have chosen—behold the body of Christ. But my friends, where is the body of Christ, seeing that outward body is now no more?' She then set forth in a very plain manner, what the body of Christ was—that it was composed of living and sanctified members, who alone could constitute a church, that will reign triumphant in Heaven. She spoke one hour and a half, and gave abundant evidence of being a gospel minister.

"We were very kindly entertained that night in the village, and on Second-day had a pleasant ride about four miles to Newport, where we had a large meeting in a school house, and the word was preached with power. Priscilla commenced with the language of Paul, 'One Lord, one faith, one baptism, one God and Father of all, who is in all, over all and through all.' Here she pointed to the great inconsistency of professing Christians contending one with another about opinions, seeing that we all profess to have the 'one Lord, one faith, one baptism.' All profess to have Christ for their Saviour—all are bound to the same eternity, and expect to be judged at the same tribunal, 'and I find,' she said, 'as I travel up and down in the land, living members of the true church of Christ, among the various professors of Christianity. And although many of these may be assailed with deep trials, in their journey toward the promised land of rest, yet, as in the outward world, it is necessary there should be day and night, heat and cold, rain and sunshine, and the various vicissitudes that occur in the outward elements, that the earth may bring forth an abundance of fruit, so in the spiritual world, it is necessary to pass through trials and tribulations, that by undergoing a fiery trial of our faith with patience, we may be made the happy partakers of divine enjoyments, even while we remain in a probationary state of being.

"The people in these parts are so unacquainted with our manner of worship, that some are very unwilling to believe that our Friends speak from immediate impressions, but rather say that they have studied all these things and prepared them beforehand; and many of them look upon our manner of silent worship as a dead form. But it may be that the day will come, when *He* who has promised to teach his people himself, will unfold to the understandings of those who now believe not, the mysteries of that kind of worship, which is not performed only in the mountain, nor yet at Jerusalem, and bring them to understand the language addressed to the woman of Samaria, 'The hour cometh and *now is*, when the true worshippers shall worship the Father, in spirit and in truth.'

"Priscilla tells the people, she does not wish to proselyte them to any one society of people; but her mission is to call them away from all sectarian prejudices and the traditions of men, 'to the word nigh in the heart and in the mouth,' that they may no longer be scattered abroad as sheep without a shepherd, on the barren mountains of an empty profession, where they are liable to be blown about, with every wind of doctrine, and the cunning craftiness of men, whereby they lay in wait to deceive.

"Priscilla's feelings of love and interest are not confined within the narrow limits of sectarianism—but to her, all denominations of people are equally near and dear, for she is aware that a true follower of the Lamb must have that mark of discipleship, by which alone they can ever be designated, 'Love one unto another.'

"We have had a large and deeply interesting meeting in a meeting house of the Seventh-day Baptists at Shiloh. I think it was the largest meeting we have had since we have been in New Jersey, except Salem Quarterly Meeting. These people who differ from many others in their form of worship appear to have the right thing at heart. Plain in their appearance, mild and deliberate in their doings among men, their hearts appear prepared to receive good, let it come from whom it may. Dear Priscilla was very much favored, her doctrine descended as the dew; and like the early and latter rain was distilled upon the tender herb. But, what shall I say of her enlargement in the house of prayer? How shall I describe the depth of that solemnity, that brought many into the fellowship of the Truth. Her service was as the beams of the morning to the weary traveller who has walked in untrodden paths through mists of darkness, and now sees unfolded, through the light of Truth, the pathway to the habitations of tranquillity."

During this visit through New Jersey, Priscilla's service was remarkable at several of the meetings which she attended. We give another circumstance as related to us, from the remembrance of a late valued friend, who knew the parties most directly interested.

"After Priscilla had been engaged for some time in gospel communication, she somewhat abruptly left the subject of her discourse, and pausing a few moments under an evident weight of painful exercise, she addressed a brother present, whom she described as holding a high position in the meeting, but yet was secretly indulging in a temptation, which if yielded to would close the door of mercy to his soul. In earnest and solemn entreaty she endeavored to awaken him to a sense of his condition, and closed by informing him that he had heretofore received an unmistakable warning, but now this was the last, and she believed his end was near.

"As this message was delivered in a meeting where there were but few members, and all well acquainted, astonishment and doubts respecting its applicability were expressed at the close, by the various groups collected around the house. One aged Friend, who had always lived in the neighborhood, thoughtfully pondered a long time on the matter while riding home with his family, and then exclaimed, 'Well, I do not believe there is such a person in our meeting!'

"But the word sent forth had accomplished that for which it was intended. The individual spoken to, confessed to his wife when the day was over, that he was the person addressed, having long been secretly indulging in the immoderate use of intoxicating drink, which had deadened his moral perceptions, and at times so overwhelming had been its depressing effects as to occasion the desire to end his life by his own hands.

"The 'warning' previously given was from a female Friend, who at the same place had spoken similar language, and after describing the individual, had with much emotion expressed surprise that she should be led to speak thus among her family and her kindred.

"This 'warning' was unheeded, but now another merciful visitation was offered and accepted, though at the eleventh hour. Short was the remaining measure of his life, and he passed away from time, testifying to the saving power of the Word of the Lord, through his chosen instrument, which word had been spoken to his soul, ere it was too late to ask and to obtain forgiveness."

After this visit through the southern and middle counties of New Jersey, our friend P. C. attended Philadelphia Yearly Meeting.

An extract from the diary of our deceased friend, E. M. Davis, dated spring of 1832, will we think be in place here as being a written testimony to the religious discernment with which Priscilla was gifted. It refers to a time of deep trial in Elizabeth's experience, wherein heavenly light seemed to be withdrawn, and she almost ready to believe she would not again know the revealings of Divine guidance. In this season of close proving our friend P. C. was made an instrument of help, and she was lifted out of the slough of despair. The extract from her diary is as follows.

"During all this period (of trial and temptation,) I never divulged my state to mortal man, but would lie awake night after night bemoaning my condition. When despair seemed to be at the very door, our friend P. C. came to Philadelphia to attend the Yearly Meeting and made her home with us.

"She told me afterwards, that during the first and second days, her suffering on my account was almost insupportable, but no door opened for relief, until Seventh-day evening, when, at her request, we retired together to her chamber; she then in a close and solemn manner disclosed her feelings concerning me. She told me she was only a messenger sent to prepare the way of the Lord, who would accomplish His own work in his own time, if I were willing to obey His will. She had much to say by way of caution and encouragement; not pointing out what I would have to do, but that which I had omitted, as being the cause of my present desolate state. I was then enabled to resign to my heavenly Father the government of my poor tossed and weary heart, and received the assurance that He would be with me and prove 'strength in weakness, riches in poverty and a present help in the needful time.'"

From Philadelphia, Priscilla went on to New York. Attended Yearly Meeting there and then proceeded to New England. The Friend who accompanied her a few months in this visit, furnishes the following account of some of her movements and services.

"6mo. 3d, 1832.—During the week of the Yearly Meeting, Priscilla Cadwallader had an evening meeting appointed at Brooklyn. Many from New York attended. Priscilla's way seemed closed; after sitting some time in silence she revealed her feelings by simply expressing these few words: 'The spirits of the prophets are subject to the prophets.' 'I feel my spirit in subjection.' Other ministering Friends then addressed the assembly. On our returning from meeting, Priscilla said there had been nothing for her to do. She believed those she wished to see were not present, neither had they been generally invited. Upon inquiry this was found to be the case. She felt comfortable in having done what she could.

"5th.—We are now on the East river, bound to Nantucket, into which quarter P. C. apprehended herself called of the Master. She had for some days been looking towards a general visit on Long Island, but this view entirely closed and the other opened, and so increased, both in clearness and weight, as to call for immediate compliance.

"7th.—An appointed meeting at New Bedford. Much valuable matter was communicated. An emphatic warning went forth to an individual present to delay no longer the work of repentance, lest the day of invitation should pass by, and he or she should not be gathered. Our friend was much favored.

"14th.—Nantucket. After having an appointed meeting, we attended their Monthly Meeting to-day. The word of encouragement went forth to the little handful of Friends living here, and the belief was expressed that as there is a withdrawal from all outward dependencies and a desire to dwell near the principle of Truth, sons will come from far and daughters from the ends of the earth, who by the powerful language of conduct will be instrumental in calling the minds of the people away from all useless forms, and in opening to their view the beauty and simplicity of that worship which is performed in spirit and in truth.

"16th.—Met the colored inhabitants of the Island to whom Priscilla felt her mind drawn. It was a season of instruction.

"17th.—In the afternoon a large meeting. P. C. was abundantly qualified to feed the hungry, clothe the naked, and refresh the thirsty soul. The truths of the gospel were clearly opened, and there was cause to believe that the ground had been prepared by the great Husbandman, at whose command the seed of the kingdom was at that time sown.

"The mind of this devoted handmaid seems peculiarly drawn to call the people home from the barren mountains of an empty profession. Great openness in the minds of those visited.

"7th mo. 3d.—Again at New Bedford. The meeting here was a season of deep exercise, though also a time of refreshment. P. felt called to testify that talents of a superior order had been bestowed upon some who were present, which had they been used in accordance with the design of Best Wisdom, would have made their possessors stars of the first magnitude in Truth's galaxy; but instead of being employed to the honor of the beneficent Giver, they are buried in an eager pursuit of the emoluments and pleasures of this world.

"5th.—We left New England for New York city. Friends met us at the wharf with the information that the cholera was prevailing there; and as Priscilla had had no view of present religious service in that city it was thought best not to land, but to proceed direct to Rahway.

"8th.—Last evening we had a meeting in the court house at Perth Amboy. The room was full and the meeting solemn. This morning, First-day, sat with Friends of Rahway, and in the afternoon went to Woodbridge to attend an appointed meeting. A large concourse assembled at the Presbyterian meeting house. P. C. cited attention to the appearance of Christ in the heart of man, where his appearance is too often disregarded; the mind being so filled with other guests, there is no room for the reception of the heavenly Visitant, which, if entertained, would bring all into the purity of the Divine nature.

"13th.—Plainfield. Friends usual meeting day; general invitation had also been given to the neighbors. After a long silence, P. merely expressed, 'When the poor servant can do *nothing*, he is not accountable for idleness. *Formerly*, when the servant was sent to water the flock, being unable to remove the stone from the well's mouth, there was no condemnation for the non-performance of the service; *so now* there is something cast in my way which I am not able to remove, whereby the pure flowing of gospel communication is obstructed.'

"22d.—For the past ten days we have had many appointed meetings, mostly from among

Friends; the congregations were large and attentive, and, at the close, satisfaction was frequently expressed with the gospel labors of our friend. It is grateful occasionally to meet with those who, though making a different outward profession, feel, and by conduct manifest, that 'in Christ all names and sects and parties fall.' This morning had a meeting at Johnsonburg, and in the afternoon another ten miles further on, in an Academy. As that was found much too small to contain those assembling, the Presbyterian minister offered his house, which was soon filled.

"24th.—We are with a Moravian family. Several of the children unite with Friends in principle; one has joined in membership with us. The nearest Friends' meeting is sixteen miles from here. It is refreshing thus unexpectedly to meet with kindred spirits. The father and mother, though bearing a different name as religious professors, received us with great kindness. We left their hospitable dwelling, and went on to Hamburg, expecting to proceed next morning. No Friends reside here.

"25th.—Early this morning P. felt her mind arrested, and could not go further till she had

had a religious opportunity with the inhabitants at this place. They assembled at their meeting house in the afternoon in accordance with her request. After deep travail she had satisfactory service. I believe there were some present, who, though they went disposed to ridicule, had to acknowledge the power of the Most High was abundantly manifest.

"29th.—Attended meeting at Cornwall by appointment. It was a season of deep exercise and trial to Priscilla, who had to testify against a spirit of rebellion or disobedience to Truth's requirements, whereby death reigned.

"31st.—Came on 40 miles to Kakiat, a remote branch of Cornwall Monthly Meeting. About four families compose a Preparative Meeting here. A considerable number collected. After a long silence Priscilla arose and expressed her belief that the way for gospel communication was closed by the unfaithfulness of some one present. An unwillingness simply to arise and lift the latch, prevented the flowing of the gospel stream, which she believed might have been even as a river to bathe in. When it was nearly time for meeting to close, she again arose and was enabled by a close and searching testimony to find some relief. This testimony came home to a young Friend present, who acknowledged there had been an unwillingness on that occasion to yield obedience to a duty that had been unfolded before her.

Passed on through Newberg, up the western side of the Hudson river, having many meetings on the way. Crossed the hills, or rather mountains, and went back towards the interior of the State, to Neversink, Thompsontown or Thompsonville, &c. At the latter place there are no Friends but one family, and one other individual. The meetings were comfortable seasons. The few under our name were encouraged to dwell so near the principle of Truth, that their conduct might bear witness, among their neighbors, to the reality and all-sufficiency of this Indwelling Power, and they were told that if faithful to their profession, they might be instrumental in drawing other minds away from the barrenness of external dependencies, home to the living spring in themselves.

"Eighth month 19th.—Have returned to the river, after having had some toilsome travel over mountains and through beech woods. To-day we have had a large and satisfactory meeting at Esopus. The table was bountifully spread with heavenly dainties.

"26th.—At Athens, N. Y. On reaching this place yesterday we were informed the cholera was prevailing to a great extent. We drove to the Friends' house where we expected to stop, and found it was in the infected district; nearly every house in the street was closed, twelve deaths having recently occurred in the square. The Friend (John Lawton) came to the door and told us how they were situated, saying, 'You are welcome, if you think it best to stop.' Priscilla was silent for a few moments, and then said, 'I am ready to get out,' which we accordingly did. John Lawton had on a former occasion travelled nine months with P. C. in the prosecution of one of her religious engagements, and he and his wife were now acting the part of good Samaritans to the sick and dying around them.

"Attended meeting here this morning. It was very large and solemn. All the meeting houses of other denominations were closed, their pastors having fled from the contagion. The inhabitants of the city generally attended our meeting and it was a memorable season.

"27th.—We had an appointed meeting at Catskill, five miles off. When we left the house of our kind friend at Athens, to go to the meeting at Catskill, his next door neighbors were living and well; when we returned in the evening, they were dead and buried. We feel serious in thus being in the midst of an infected district, but believing we are right in being here, we both are satisfied, let the event be as it may.

"31st.—Coeymans. J. L. accompanied us to this place. On our arrival P. felt her mind drawn in gospel love to have an evening meeting appointed at Coxsackie, a village five miles distant, where there are no Friends. Some discouragements were thrown in the way by the Friend to whom the concern was mentioned. He said there was no openness *there* to receive such a visit, but he would willingly make arrangements for a meeting about a mile from the place designated. Priscilla replied, she 'had nothing to do at the town he mentioned; she would be glad to have one at Coxsackie, but if he was unwilling the effort should be made, she would rest her burden upon him.' At this juncture J. L. came in, and at once offered to give all needful attention to the matter. The Friend went with him, and on going to Coxsackie they found no difficulty in making satisfactory arrangements for a meeting. In the evening we had a large gathering. While the people were collecting, much lightness and idle curiosity were visible, but soon silence prevailed, and the minds of all appeared solemnized. I think it may truly be said, truth reigned triumphantly, and that this devoted handmaid has abundant cause to thank God and take fresh courage. Although most of those present were entirely unaccustomed to Friends' usages, and there were more present than could find seats, no impatience was manifested during the silent part of the meeting, and much satisfaction was expressed at the close.

"Ninth month 2d.—At Staunton Hill meeting we had a very large gathering of other societies. The deportment of the people showed that their attention was measurably centered to the Witness within themselves, and they were thus enabled to receive the word handed them by our dedicated friend, who was eminently favored.

"3d.—Had a meeting at a small settlement about five miles distant from Thomas Nelson's, where we lodged last night. The neighbors generally collected. A very trying meeting to Priscilla, who had very close doctrine to deliver, and a very solemn warning to sound to some present, who scoffed at and reviled the way of salvation, as acknowledged by the Society of Friends. The people were called to the Indwelling Power of the Highest, or Christ within, which was shown to be 'the way, the Truth, and the life.'

"5th.—Meeting at Rensselaerville. Had the acceptable company of our friend, Ruth Spencer, sister to Job Scott.

"6th.—Bethlehem, N. Y. For some days past the time has seemed near for my release from my present engagement as Priscilla's companion. On reaching Berne, we found Martha Rushmore prepared for such a service. I now purpose turning my face homeward. The prospect of leaving this dear friend and mother thus among strangers is a trying one; but my mind is comforted by the presentation of the language, 'what avails thy presence to one who is under my protecting care.' Surely His power, which has abundantly proved to be her battle-axe, her shield, and her exceeding great reward, through many and deep exercises, will continue with her to the end of her arduous undertaking."

The fall and winter of 1832, and some months of 1833, were spent by Priscilla in Scipio, N. Y. Much of this time she was suffering under severe indisposition. An extract from a letter written by our friend, A. P., of Western New York, gives an interesting picture of her Christian patience, and cheerfulness, under this trying allotment.

"In 1832 and 1833 we were the glad recipients of a religious visit from Priscilla Cadwallader, and we were deeply impressed with her devotion and purity of purpose. After attending and appointing meetings in most parts of Scipio Monthly Meeting, she was taken sick at the house of our kind friends, J. and F. F., where she remained about four weeks. She was then taken to F. and M. A.'s, where she was very kindly and tenderly cared for, for three months. In the winter, when a little better and able to be removed, we invited her to come to us. She came and remained under our roof about seven months, during which time she was mostly confined to her bed, and, at times, a great sufferer, her pain sometimes being very acute. But her spirit was always beautifully serene and quiet. Never a murmur escaped her lips; neither a dissatisfied look nor gesture. It was then we learned to love and appreciate her value in private life, for she was ever cheerful and instructive in conversation, when alone with our family circle, though often somewhat reserved when strangers were present. We all found it a privilege far beyond the common opportunities of life to wait on her, and I have no words to express fully our love and admiration."

We have no reliable information of Priscilla's movements from the date of the fore-mentioned severe attack of indisposition, until Sixth mo. 1834, when she thus wrote to her husband from Uxbridge, Upper Canada.

"Once more feeling a little strength and ability to write, I shall endeavor to give thee a sketch of my travels since my companion wrote thee last. We left Pelham and travelled West about 400 miles, visiting the towns and inhabitants between Pelham and London; and since, we have been travelling N. E., and are now about half way between Yonge Street and Pickering. How much further North and East I shall have to go, is yet concealed from me, therefore must leave that to Him who knows what is best, and how far to lead so feeble a being, who can live where the good Master is pleased to lead; and I find He is always present to enable me to do whatever he requires at my hands. I have none other to look unto nor to spread my cause before, but God my Redeemer, in whom I trust, and find rest, let the tribulations of this world be ever so great. He ofttimes lifts me up to ride with Him in the chariot of Love, and it is the breathing of my heart that thou mayest enjoy the same, through faithful walking, and stand prepared to hear the last trump with joy."

No further notice of this visit to Canada has been obtained. On her return to the States, she was again prostrated upon a bed of sickness, in Mendon, at the house of E. and N. A. A Friend says:

"When Genesee Yearly Meeting came on, though still sick in bed, she felt drawn to go to Farmington, and was able to visit both men's and women's meetings, and to deliver in each the message with which she believed herself intrusted. In the women's meeting, she spoke beautifully and impressively of that divine love that had inspired her soul, and given her strength to arise from her sick bed to come and sit with us. In the men's meeting they were engaged in the consideration of a revision of our discipline, and she exhorted them to great care therein, and to seek for divine guidance in reference to every proposed change, lest they should inadvertently put it in the power of some to oppress others, and thereby obstruct that growth which Truth would sanction.

"She remained at Farmington during the remainder of the Yearly Meeting week, but was only able to attend one other meeting. This was the public meeting held on Fourth day. She then spoke interestingly to a very quiet, though very crowded audience. At this meeting she predicted our present national conflict, saying: 'I hear the cannon's roar, and the beating of drums, and I see the horse and his rider amid the clash of arms and pools of human blood. Oh, Carolina! Carolina! how I would gather thee as a hen gathers her chickens, but thou wilt not hear the call. Slavery will go down sooner or later, and I entreat *you* to wash your hands in innocency.'

"About this time my husband and I took an opportunity to go and sit alone by her, when she told us she had been *trying* to go home, until she had *lost almost all her strength;* whenever she looked that way, she saw *nothing* but *darkness* and *dismay*, and she knew of no better way than to *dwell in the light*, even if she lost all of *this world's friendship* thereby."

Her long absence from home was the occasion of much uneasiness and painful surmisings among some of the Friends of her own Yearly Meeting. They, perhaps, were not aware of all the attending circumstances, including her many severe and tedious attacks of sickness. On one occasion, when on a sick bed, to which she had been confined several months, a letter was received expressing this dissatisfaction. This was a great stroke to her, but she bore it quietly, merely remarking, "I have striven hard to make the cloak of charity large enough to cover it."

She was at one time confined by sickness at the house of her kind friends, C. and P. F. After one of these severe attacks of indisposition, a friend inquired where she had been all this long time?—intimating she had been almost forgotten. Priscilla meekly replied: "In the hollow of the good Hand."

In a letter written by B. U., of Henrietta, Monroe county, New York, Tenth month 24th, 1835, to Priscilla's husband and son-in-law, are the following remarks:

"The stay in this country of our much beloved friend, your dear Priscilla Cadwallader, seems to be remarkably protracted. I willingly devote a few moments to inform you of her getting along since our last Genesee Yearly Meeting, in the Sixth month, 1835, which she attended. She was then in a comfortable state of health, which she had recovered after many months sickness, of which you have had the particulars. At our Yearly Meeting, Friends expressed much unity and sympathy with her, as noticed in the Epistle to the Indiana Yearly Meeting. After which she again commenced traveling in the prosecution of her religious labors, although she had taken a heavy cold which settled on her lungs, but she continued to travel among Friends and others, in some places visiting the families of many different persuasions. She was cordially received by them, and very great openness was manifested towards her; and her labors of love under the anointing power of the Truth, on which her mind seemed to be centered, were often refreshing to many minds, and bore evidence that she realized the fulfilment of the ancient promise, 'Lo, I am with you alway.'"

The Friend, at whose house she had been confined several months by severe indisposition, speaking of Priscilla's long visit in their neighborhood, says:

"I think it right to notice her sudden release from further labor in this part of the country, and her hasty departure for home, after her long absence.

"My husband was taking her and her companion to Farmington, she having a prospect of visiting the families there; after riding several miles in silence, Priscilla said: 'Isaac, thou mayst turn back; I am released from the service, and at liberty to go home.' This unexpected releasement was so welcome to her, we could hardly persuade her to stay one night longer. Next morning she left us."

The following Testimony, issued by Junius Monthly Meeting, soon after her return home, and addressed to her Monthly Meeting, possesses an interest which gives it a place in this memoir. It shows the esteem in which she was held by those Friends, among whom she was often detained months at a time by illness:

"To Blue River Monthly Meeting of Friends, Indiana:

"Dear Friends,—Our beloved Friend, Priscilla Cadwallader, having been long absent from you, in the prosecution of her religious visit, and during a considerable portion of the time which has elapsed, her lot having been cast within the limits of this Yearly Meeting, (Genesee,) where also she was long confined by bodily indisposition, we deem it right to inform you that her health being restored, she spent several weeks the past summer in this neighborhood, held a number of public meetings, and visited the families belonging to this meeting, in all which her services have been truly satisfactory; her conversation among us has been such as becometh the gospel, and her ministry living and edifying. Having returned again to her outward abode with you, our prayers accompany her, that the care of the Shepherd of Israel, which has been vouchsafed in the restoration of her health and her preservation in the life of Truth, may continue to be abundantly her experience; and in that love which binds together the Lord's children everywhere, we commend her, as a sister beloved, to your sympathy, Christian fellowship, and unabated affectionate regard.

"Signed by direction and on behalf of Junius Monthly Meeting of Friends, in the State of New York, held Second month 21st, 1838.

WEBSTER LAING,
DEANNA BONNEL, } Clerks."

In 1839 she obtained a minute to visit Friends and others, within the verge of Indiana Yearly Meeting, which service was performed.

In 1846 another minute was obtained for religious service within the limits of Blue River Quarterly Meeting. This service was also performed. We have no *particulars* of either journey.

In 1850 a minute was received to visit the meetings constituting Baltimore and Ohio Yearly Meetings, and also some belonging to Philadelphia and New York Yearly Meetings. We have no account of her visit in Ohio, and but little of her labors within the limits of Baltimore Yearly Meeting, only that she was in Loudon county, Virginia, in the Eleventh month of 1850.

A Friend who travelled with her as companion in a subsequent part of this journey, has furnished a record of it, portions of which we extract.

It may be well to remark, in this connection, that in making extracts from the few journals that have been available, while we have omitted much that no doubt would have interested many of our readers, we have endeavored to select such parts as most clearly show the character of our friend's labors. To avoid being prolix, we also have omitted in most cases, the names of persons by whom she has been kindly entertained.

"Twelfth month 29th, 1850.—On First-day morning we were at Little Britain meeting. Priscilla spoke clearly and satisfactorily on the subject of woman's preaching. After the meeting had been some time settled, she said in a low voice, without rising from her seat, 'Withholding more than is meet tendeth to poverty.' Upon which a friend arose and said a few words. After meeting Priscilla told this friend she was sensible she had something to offer, but was disposed to withhold it; had she done so, her (P.'s) way would have been closed.

"31st. West Nottingham.—We had a close searching time. Hypocrisy and a persecuting and envious spirit were testified against. Christian love was beautifully explained, and the people were called to the principle of light and life within, which would redeem from every sin. This meeting closed after a touching prayer.

"First month 5th.—Information having been

given, the meeting at New Garden was large. After a powerful communication, P. C. bowed the knee with this language: 'Wilt thou, O Father! show mercy unto this people. Thy handmaid heareth the strife of swords and the clashing of tongues.' On coming into this neighborhood, an unusual weight of exercise rested on Priscilla. This was somewhat relieved after the attendance of this meeting, but she found it would be safest for her to attend the Monthly Meetings belonging to the Western Quarter, as they came in course.

"In the attendance of these meetings, P. C. was often engaged to call the people home to the pure love of the everlasting Gospel, which would restrain them from all strife and contention. Her testimonies in the different meetings to the importance of *home work* were powerful and impressive; and her addresses to individual states with which she had to feel, bore evidence that she was qualified to sit where the people sat. On one occasion, under a sense that the gospel stream was obstructed, the enquiry was solemnly sounded, 'who hath filled Jacob's well with trash, that so the pure water of life cannot rise?' The obstruction was shown to be *contention about doctrines, and watching over our neighbor's garden to the neglect of our own.* Those who were tempted to look upon prayer as a needless or formal thing, were counselled to draw near to the fountain of Light and Love, and in humble prostration before Him who is the alone source of wisdom, seek for that spirit which is 'first pure, then peaceable, and easy to be entreated.' She repeatedly testified, that as this Divine power is submitted to, it will preserve from envy, backbiting, and every feeling that would separate brother from brother, and sister from sister. The reverse of thus dwelling in unity and brotherly kindness was clearly portrayed, and that its effect would be 'to divide in Jacob and scatter in Israel.' But she believed there were those who would be able to stand firmly upon the sea of glass that John saw, mingled with fire, having the harps of God in their hands. This view cheered her on her way, and strengthened her to call her endeared brothers and sisters to that principle which would ensure their everlasting peace. Under the spirit of supplication which often remarkably rested upon her, she fervently petitioned that He who ruleth in the hearts of his children, 'would bring the wanderers back from the barren mountains into the green pastures of life, even to that valley where the dew lies long and the grass is forever green.'"

In 1851 and 1852 Priscilla visited many of the meetings within the limits of Philadelphia Yearly Meeting, and the families of Friends belonging to the three Monthly Meetings in Philadelphia.

Our valued friend, the late Samuel Comfort, a short time before his death, furnished the following memorandum, which refers to two meetings held in his neighborhood, during the prosecution of the visit now before us:

"Tenth month 17th, 1851.—We went with Priscilla Cadwallader and companions to meeting,—a full meeting. Priscilla, after a considerable time of silence, and deep spiritual travail, spoke in the demonstration of the Spirit and with power many gospel truths,—not speculative but practical,—beginning with these words: 'Who shall speak in the name of the Lord?' enlarging upon the view that our God is a consuming fire;—that he consumes sin in the obedient soul;—

that none but those who are obedient to his law, and have known him to consume sin by the baptism of the Holy Ghost and fire in the soul, can speak in the name of the Lord;—that obedience was all He required;—that it was disobedience which expelled man from Eden;—that Eden could not be regained nor enjoyed but by obedience, the obedience of Christ Jesus, the blessed example and way to the Father;—that reason, though a noble gift, could not know God, but by divine illumination and revelation;—that Christ was the tree of Life in the midst of the garden;—that the believing and obedient freely partake of the fruit;—that the *flaming sword* at the east of the garden was the *love of God*, to cut down and consume, or burn up all the transgressing nature—*all sin in the soul*, and subject all the propensities of man's mind and will to the will of God.' These subjects were extensively spoken of and illustrated.

"18th.—My wife and I, and our M., went to P. C.'s meeting, appointed at Pennsbury, at 3 P. M. She preached the gospel of salvation; had a sense given her of the state of the members of the meeting, and was much favored in bearing testimony to the Truth, inviting to obedience, and warning against disregarding and rejecting the offers of divine love and mercy. After a long and interesting communication, she bowed in solemn supplication."

During most of Priscilla's labors within the limits of Philadelphia Yearly Meeting, at this time, our esteemed friend, the late Hannah Lukens, whose humility and devotion of life justly endeared her to many, was her sympathising companion. From the memoranda which she occasionally made we have been allowed to make extracts.

The account is not continuous, but it shows the nature of the services in which they were engaged, and embraces the time of the foregoing record of our friend, S. C. There are also but few dates given, enough, however, to enable us to decide the time when these meetings were visited.

"Second month, 1851.—Left home to attend the Southern Quarter, as companion to P. C. The first meeting we attended was Appoquinamink. The small house was well filled, and we had a good meeting. Most of those present were not Friends, and they told us there were but four men who were members;—no woman Friend belonged there; and the meeting was often attended by only one man, and sometimes his little son, seven years old,—a remarkable child, lately deceased. The Quarterly Meeting held three days;—was small, but very comfortable. Many of the Friends came a great distance to attend. Our home was at Sarah Cowgill's, a dear old Friend, aged 88 years, but bright and lively as though it was still the days of her youth. When we arrived at the house, she was standing on the porch; some one said, 'this is Hannah Lukens.' She said, 'not Mary Lukens' daughter?' When told it was, she took me earnestly by the hand and said: 'Oh! come in,—that dear good woman,—I never expected to see one of her children. Oh! how I loved her.' Sarah Cowgill was so kind and so much interested in the company of her friends, that she made me think many times of my dear mother. She seemed so alive in the Truth and in best things. We had an evening meeting at Camden, and at the Neck. At the latter, P. began with saying, 'The Lord loves all—the high and the low, the rich and the poor. He loves the poorest beggar who begs his bread from door to door equally with the king on his throne.' She proceeded in a way that attracted the serious attention of every one, and her prayer was so affecting, that it seemed a very solemn meeting. Centre came next. It was a favored time. I thought the feeling was enough to soften the hardest heart. But, as she told me afterwards, when she first stood up, she felt there was great opposition to the principle, and she had hard work for a time. I said in my heart, surely the faithful will be clear. It was very grateful to my feelings to be present at these meetings. Pine Grove and Snow Hill meetings were both attended, and were favored seasons. Things were laid down (or opened) so plainly, that a child of ten years old could understand them. At Easton had a large meeting. It was a very ancient place, and looked like such an one. They told us that George Fox and Wm. Penn had held meetings there, though not in the same house. This made me take more notice of the places. These dear, good men, who have long gone before, and left us such a bright example of justice, mercy, forbearance, and loving-kindness,—they were faithful in their day, and the remembrance thereof seemed to create anew the desire that we of the present day may be alike faithful to what may be our part and measure to fill up. Having attended all the meetings that were laid out for us, Priscilla says she cannot see any way further at present. We are here at J. D.'s, and feel very comfortable, waiting to see which way we are to go next. Oh, it is good for us to wait, and trust, and feel our dependent state, as we go along from day to day. I have been glad to be with Priscilla. I have never looked back with regret, but have felt many times that I was in my place, though often feeling great weakness every way, and as a very little one: but blessed be the holy One, He was near to comfort me. At Bayside we had a good meeting among the Methodists. They were very attentive, and seemed grateful for the favor. Here we staid one night: it was very cold, being so near the water. When I rose in the morning and looked out at the waves rolling and foaming, all white as far as the eye could reach, I said in my heart, how grand and magnificent are the works of the Almighty hand, which made the sea and the dry land. Who can but praise Him! Priscilla feels the weight of her concern almost continuously. She seems to be in her place, and I have thought will do much good in gathering poor souls from earth to heaven. A blessed work! May it prosper. Next attended Tuckahoe and Chestertown meetings, and several others. Priscilla had to repeat the language many times, 'Come out of all noise and contention, and the strife of words; come home, come home to the Father's house.' The feeling was so solemn and impressive, that I could but desire that the call might be heard from one end of the earth to the other; or, as she expressed it, 'from the North to the South pole,' that all might be gathered to the one fold of eternal rest and peace.

"Third month.—Have returned home. Feel comfortable and satisfied with my little journey, and. grateful for the favor of being at these meetings, and other opportunities we have had together."

"I again left home in Eighth month, 1851. Met Priscilla Cadwallader in Philadelphia;—went next day to Wm. G.'s, in New Jersey, where we staid several days, Priscilla not being well. They were very kind to us. I hardly knew how to receive so much kindness, without the power of returning something back. On First-day we were at two neighboring meetings. In the afternoon P. had much to say to some one present, who did not believe there was a God. Her address was very serious and awful. She said there was a very short time between him and eternity, and encouraged him to set about immediately the great work, that he might attain a state of everlasting rest and peace, adding, there is time enough and none to spare. I cannot describe the attendant feeling, nor express the language fully. On our way to Woodstown we were at several meetings, and attended the Quarterly Meeting, which was large, and very satisfactory. Next at Greenwich, and a more favored season we have not had as yet. Priscilla had much to say to a state of lukewarmness, wherein some one was resting at ease, saying, 'things are pretty well with me. A little more sleep, a little more slumber.' The call went forth, 'awake, awake thou that sleepest, and Christ shall give thee light.' P. was much favored to speak that which appeared to claim the serious attention of all. She said the time was coming when the true church will come up out of the wilderness, clear as the sun, fair as the moon, and terrible as an army with banners; when all the false heavens and false earth will be shaken; while those who have the name, but are not living near the principle of Truth in themselves, will little by little fall away.

"Tenth month 1st.—Arrived at Reading, winding around the hills and mountains, so beautiful to behold. Our road lay along the Schuylkill river, and up a steep mountain. I believe it was the very spot I passed many years ago, with my dear parents, who are now no more. I silently reflected on it, as I rode along, it having been twenty years ago. Thanks arose in my heart, that I had been protected and cared for until the present time, by Him who careth for the sparrows, and hears the ravens when they cry. Oh, give thanks unto Him, for his mercies endure forever. Had a large evening meeting at Reading. Staid two nights at John James's, and then went to Stroudsburg. A small meeting house here, but well filled with different persuasions. All were brought into silence, and the blessed Master was pleased to be in the midst. It was an humbling season. The precious feeling that covered the meeting, I felt all the day as we rode along. At Richland it was no less a favored season. It may be said, as was formerly, Truth reigned over all—blessed be the holy name. Next at Kingwood. All of these last meetings seem to be very much as the outskirts and bye-places, among the rocks and mountains. In many of these remote places we find the sincere in heart endeavoring to live near the principle of Truth. At Solebury, Priscilla told them never to be afraid of silence, nor ashamed of the Truth. She spoke to those who sometimes have to speak to others. She said: 'We have nothing to give, until we have something given us; and if we attempt to give any thing of ourselves, it is only filthy rags.' Then attended the other meetings of Bucks Quarter. Some of these were exercising seasons. In one, the language was uttered: 'What is the matter? There is something among you that will scatter and divide, unless you come out of it. Come out of Babylon;—come out of confusion and the strife of words, oh my people.' I hardly ever heard such preaching; and it seemed to solemnize all present. At Rancocas meeting, within the limits of Burlington Quarter, Priscilla began with the query, 'What is the matter, Friends? Afraid of silence? Silence is the loudest preaching we can have.' She spoke to the people for some time, in a very feeling, close manner. Next to the Mount meeting; truly I thought we had come to the mount that might be touched; and I believe many hearts were touched with the feeling of goodness this day.

"We are now within the limits of Abington Quarter. At Byberry meeting—a close exercising time. We went to the house where dear John Comly lived, and they took us into the sitting room where he spent much of his time, when at home. There were his arm-chair and his desk, with some books, pen, ink and paper on it, just as he had used it. All around looked so plain, and seemed so serene and quiet. It was very pleasant being there, it so reminded me of him. I always loved him.

"Eleventh month, 1851.—At Rahway Quarter. Priscilla began by saying, Watchman, what of the night, repeating it several times, and then queried, 'have you been engaged to keep the watch, or have you neglected it, and let in the enemy, the world, and the things of it?' At Randolph meeting she queried: 'Who is this that drinketh in scorn like water, and maketh light of Truth, and casteth it down under-foot?' Much more was said in a very feeling and close manner. I was glad I was there. There are but very few Friends in this corner of the world. But it is said, 'they that fear God and work righteousness, are accepted with Him;' and I believe they will come from the East and the West, from the North and the South, and shall sit down in heavenly places, and there will be one fold and one shepherd.

"After being at home a little while, I engaged with dear Priscilla in visiting the families of Friends in Philadelphia. The service is only partly performed, her poor health requiring her to lay by for a while. In the right time I trust we will be able to move on again. The Lord's time is the right time."

When Priscilla was ready to proceed, her faithful companion, H. L, joined her, and they went on to the completion of the visit without further interruption. The nature of such an engagement interferes with keeping a daily record of the visits made,—thus we have no account of them.

Some notice of the opening of this concern upon the mind of our friend P. C., will, we think, be in place here. The facts connected with it, show her dependence for daily guidance on the secret pointings of the divine finger, and for which she wearied not *in waiting*, neither was she found hastening into action, by yielding to the judgment of those, who, sometimes, in all honesty, would think they could see for her. She felt she must *see for herself* before she ventured to take one step in the prosecution of her religious engagements; and although sometimes it would seem that she *waited long*, yet when light broke forth, there was a clearness of vision that left no room for doubt, and amply repaid the humble, child-like confidence of her trusting spirit.

When she came to this city, (Philadelphia,) in the fall or winter of 1851, it was under a sense of divine requirement, but without knowing what special service was before her.

Two weeks were spent in quiet retirement, at the house of the writer of this sketch, during which time her mind appeared much released from exercise. She would sometimes say, "she knew not why it was so, but she had no fears. She believed all would be right;—and perhaps she was about being released from further service." But the prospect of visiting the families of the three Monthly Meetings of Friends here, now opened upon her mind, and was received by her with a feeling of sweet submission and trust in the sufficiency of Him who put her forth, and she entered upon the arduous undertaking with a cheerful spirit and a willing heart. This labor of love and duty was not unattended by trials and discouragements, but the seal of her ministrations so remained with many of the families visited, that the acknowledgment was afterwards made, "Verily the Lord was in it, though we knew it not." This visit seemed to many, emphatically a loving farewell.

We find from the records of Blue River

Monthly Meeting, that the minute which had been given to our friend in 1850, was "returned in 1853. Labors not fully accomplished. Minute renewed with like prospect. Returned finally in 1857."

After this renewal of her minute in 1853, she was engaged in religious service in Virginia. Of this visit we have no particulars further than that she visited the meetings and many of the families in that State and Maryland. Our beloved friend was often led into the service of family visiting. The meekness, humility, and simplicity which conspicuously marked her every day deportment, were especially evidenced when thus engaged; and as she passed from house to house, the blessing of the solitary in families, and of him who was ready to perish, rested upon her and her ministrations of love. A secret sense of this was often as a brook by the way, and refreshed her spirit in the course of her exercising journey.

In 1854 Priscilla again attended Philadelphia Yearly Meeting. We extract from H. Lukens' memoranda, her testimony of P.'s services therein:

"The first sitting on Seventh-day morning was very comforting; enough so to pay me for coming. I thought we were advancing a little, and if it be only one step, if it be in the right way, it is cause of encouragement. The feeling over the meeting at times was very precious. Many living testimonies were borne to the Truth, and none more living than dear P. C.'s. It was clear and impressive, and had great weight. Oh! I thought, if we could only keep under the covering that was then over us, we could not err nor go from the right way. I believe it had a tendency to strengthen us during the several sittings of the Yearly Meeting. Let us give thanks, and take fresh courage."

The next items we have connected with this visit, are from the pen of A. P., of Western New York. They claim a place in this memoir, and show that the Christian charity and liberality of feeling to which she was concerned to call others, were exemplified in her own conduct:

"In 1855, P. C. came again with a minute of the unity of her Monthly Meeting, and visited the meetings all through this country; and although my husband and I had, in accordance with our vision of light and Truth, withdrawn our right of membership from the Society of Friends, and consequently were much shut out from even social communion with its members, she came to our house with the same loving freedom as before, thus practically evidencing the truth of what she had often declared, that she was no sectarian in spirit. Afterwards when she came again and visited the families of Friends in this meeting, she included us in her mission of love. During this religious opportunity, the few words spoken expressed a sweet peace and satisfaction in thus mingling with us.

"At one meeting during her visit to this part of the country, she particularized an individual present, whose gold had become his god. She said he had obtained large possessions, and much of it had been gained by taking advantage of the rich and grinding the face of the poor. She entreated him to stop in his career and repair the injuries he had done, or the time would come when he would have to feel that 'every man's hand was against him, and he would not only be obliged to hide in the caves and hollows of the earth from the sight of his fellow-men, but would call upon the rocks and mountains to cover him from the sight of the All-seeing eye of Justice, Mercy and Truth. And when all was gone from his grasp, what poverty of soul would he feel.' One to whom the description applied, seemed for a time to realize that he was the person spoken to, but after struggling several weeks with his convictions, he reasoned them away and went on as before; but he has long since realized the truth of all she said, and after skulking and hiding in different places for some time, not daring to go home to his beautiful mansion, he was obliged to go to another part of the country to save his life."

The minute with which she was now travelling was the last one obtained, and was returned in 1857.

The latter years of Priscilla Cadwallader's life were spent with a beloved and only daughter.

A lively interest was manifested in the welfare and happiness of the large family of children now around her, by aiding in their education, and showing a deep concern that they should by precept and example, have a careful and guarded training.

Her home was about a mile from the meeting house, and when bodily strength permitted, she always assembled there with her Friends at the hour appointed for divine worship; often walking when she had no other means of going.

In the Third month, 1859, her health visibly failed, but in the Eighth month, though scarcely able to walk alone, she rode 120 miles to attend her Quarterly Meeting, from which she returned home much improved, but still very feeble.

In the following Ninth month she felt a concern to attend her Yearly Meeting at Richmond, Ind., 140 miles distant. Though weak in body, she was strong in faith. She was unable to attend all the sittings, but her mind was bright and unimpaired, and her gospel labors at the closing opportunity were especially impressive and satisfactory to her friends. This, we believe, was the last time she was able to sit with her friends in a religious meeting. Her social converse during the week was cheerful, composed and innocent. After the Yearly Meeting was over, her friends urged her to remain awhile with them as a means of improving her health; but she thought best to return to her daughter's, remarking afterwards, "she would rather come home and die among her children," expressing a belief that her day's work was nearly accomplished.

A few weeks after her return to her family, on awaking one morning from sleep, she complained of a general coldness, and in about an hour, on the morning of the 13th of Eleventh month, 1859, she quietly departed from this world, at peace with God and man.

Note.—We close the memoir of our beloved friend under the feeling that we have not given as full an account of her travels and labors as would be desirable. We believe there are very many incidents of interest connected with her life, that are not here recorded,—but we have done the best we could, with our limited knowledge of her movements and the material at our command.

www.ingramcontent.com/pod-product-compliance
Lightning Source LLC
LaVergne TN
LVHW021413110826
845150LV00007B/1908
9781425510664